The 10 Best-Ever Anxiety Management Techniques

Workbook

The 10 Best-Ever Anxiety Management Techniques

Workbook

SECOND EDITION

Margaret Wehrenberg

W. W. Norton & Company

Independent Publishers Since 1923

New York • London

Note to Readers: Standards of clinical practice and protocol change over time, and no technique or recommendation is guaranteed to be safe or effective in all circumstances. This volume is intended as a general information resource for professionals practicing in the field of psychotherapy and mental health; it is not a substitute for appropriate training, peer review, and/or clinical supervision. Neither the publisher nor the author(s) can guarantee the complete accuracy, efficacy, or appropriateness of any particular recommendation in every respect.

For information about permission to reproduce selections from this book, write to
Permissions, W. W. Norton & Company, Inc., 500 Fifth Avenue, New York, NY 10110

For information about special discounts for bulk purchases, please contact
W. W. Norton Special Sales at specialsales@wwnorton.com or 800-233-4830

Manufacturing by LSC Harrisonburg
Production manager: Christine Critelli

Library of Congress Cataloging-in-Publication Data

Names: Wehrenberg, Margaret, author.
Title: The 10 best-ever anxiety management techniques workbook / Margaret Wehrenberg.
Other titles: Ten best-ever anxiety management techniques workbook
Description: Second edition. | New York: W.W. Norton & Company, [2018] | Series: A Norton
professional book | Includes bibliographical references and index.
Identifiers: LCCN 2017050781 | ISBN 9780393712162 (pbk.)
Subjects: LCSH: Anxiety. | Anxiety—Treatment.
Classification: LCC BF575.A6 W443 2018 | DDC 152.4/6—dc23 LC record
available at https://lccn.loc.gov/2017050781

W. W. Norton & Company, Inc.
500 Fifth Avenue, New York, N.Y. 10110
www.wwnorton.com

W. W. Norton & Company Ltd.
15 Carlisle Street, London W1D 3BS

1 2 3 4 5 6 7 8 9 0

For My Safety Net:
This whole, big, supportive and smart Family

Contents

PART IV: **MANAGING ANXIOUS BEHAVIOR**

Acknowledgments

My association with W. W. Norton began over a decade ago, and I have had the privilege to work with some exceptional editors. This is my second project with Ben Yarling and my first with Deborah Malmud, and I must add them to the list of people who have been not only instrumental but also necessary. Thanks to them for motivating and challenging me, and thanks especially for shaping the work with your knowledge and counsel. I also want to thank the entire Norton team, who are so responsive and helpful—everyone who has worked behind the scenes and made it possible for me to bring this information to the public.

No one works in a vacuum, but for a professional in private practice, outside academia and agencies, I have been blessed beyond words with an association of professionals who are also dear friends. Psychologists, social workers, counselors, writers, educators, consultants: you all make me better. I learn professionally from you every day, and I grow personally from our conversations. My heartfelt appreciation goes to Susan Cherwien, Shannon Burns, Cathy Lessmann, Linda Lee, Mary Jane Murphy-Gonzales, Laurel Coppersmith, Nancy Hoffman, Sandra Faulkner, Lurlene McDaniel, Mary Lou Carney, Martha Straus, and Yonah Klem. I must also include some of the men who go with this crowd of amazing women whose conversation and encouragement are so meaningful: David Cherwien, Paul Lee, Gary Lessmann, and, of course, Paul Bauermeister and the many Mikes.

I know it is appropriate to thanks one's family, but seriously, my amazing daughter, Elowyn Proffer, listens, reflects, and offers such sage advice. I can never get over how she got so wise about people and business. And my son, Hal Wehrenberg, who is always up for an in-depth discussion of books and movies, for which we share a love, is too far away, so I have to appreciate not only him but also the technology that lets us see each other while we chat. Wes Proffer, who knows something about everything, and Jessica Wehrenberg, who is one smart woman with a great sense of humor, always delight me with their insights. But the joy-and-elation category belongs to the grandchildren these days. It is Max who brings delight into my life, and Sloan—you have the best giggle! You brighten up any day that I get to see you. And newborn Quinn: I can't wait to get to know you.

Finally, I want to express how deeply appreciative I am of the clients who have worked with me over the years, who tried ideas that blossomed into techniques that were refined with their work. I am dedicating this volume to you.

The 10 Best-Ever Anxiety Management Techniques

Workbook

Introduction

As I revised *The 10 Best-Ever Anxiety Management Techniques*, it seemed to also be the right time to revise this workbook, meant as a companion to guide the implementation and practice of the 10 techniques and the many methods they comprise. Burgeoning research in psychotherapy and brain science affects the presentation of these techniques; it continues to support methods included in the previous edition, but new information about memory reconsolidation in particular will be reshaping social anxiety treatment in our society.

This workbook provides both structure and clarification on how to make the techniques work. Chapters coincide with those in *The 10 Best-Ever Anxiety Management Techniques* but use charts, worksheets, and self-assessment tools to will help readers see the effects of their anxiety. The checklists and self-assessments are based on situations I have observed over the years in my practice. As such, they are not validated tests but rather represent questions I ask my clients and the circumstances they describe to me.

These simple assessments are followed by several methods that will correct the type of anxiety you are experiencing. Some people will benefit from working through all the techniques, whereas others will need only a few to master the anxiety in their lives.

An added component to the workbook is an option to download an audio file with 10 methods that complement the 10 techniques. You will be able to practice methods of breathing, mindfulness, and relaxation with audio guidance as you listen. You can find these files at margaretwehrenberg.com/audiotracks.

Homework assignments within and at the end of each technique chapter are written so that you can fill them out in the book. Research has suggested that concrete homework assignments such as these keep your focus on your goals and thus increase the benefits of trying the methods. They also increase your mastery of techniques that will move you toward your ultimate goal of lifelong ability to manage anxiety. If you are working with a therapist, these homework assignments also ensure that you and your therapist are on the same page about what your goals are and how to achieve them. Without the clarity of homework, both of you may lose sight of them.

Those assignments will be S.I.M.P.L.E., which stands for the process of planning. Identify the *situation*, note the *impact* it has on your life, clarify the *method* you are going to use, *practice* your plan, set goals for *lifework*, and *evaluate* how it works or should be modified.

I am well aware that many people have serious mental health conditions in addition to anxiety. My intent is not to solve every problem but rather to make it easier for you to move forward regardless, freed from debilitating anxiety symptoms. If anxiety has originated in trauma or difficult experiences during early life, those conditions require more help than is available in this workbook. If your anxiety is severe or persistent, you may well need the advice and support of a psychotherapist to work through your symptoms. However, improving your confidence in your ability to manage anxiety symptoms will make other mental health concerns easier to deal with. It is my hope that when you follow these techniques for managing your anxiety symptoms, you will experience a relief you never knew was possible.

PART I

Assess Yourself

ONE

What Kind of Anxiety Do You Have?

Anxiety. Stress. Worry. Panic. These words get thrown around a lot in everyday language, and people use them to refer to a wide range of feelings and experiences. But in the clinical sense, these terms have specific definitions with critical differences.

Stress is a condition everyone knows. When challenges come our way, we respond with physical and mental reactions aimed at tolerating and resolving the stress. Not all stress is bad; a certain amount can promote growth. For instance, a challenging project at work might help you improve your organizational skills and expand your creativity. That kind of stress could be called "eustress"—as opposed to "distress," which is what most of us mean when we talk about stress. "Distress" occurs when we are faced with something too challenging or even overwhelming, causing us physical tension and mental anguish.

Anxiety can create stress or be a response to it. Anxiety is the experience every person has in response to ambiguity. When we are uncertain, we feel a certain sensation in our gut, and our thoughts turn toward figuring it out. We begin "what-if" thinking—"What if _____ happens? What if I _____?"—as a means to figure out the ambiguity and resolve our anxiety.

When we feel anxiety in the absence of an actual problem, "what-if" thinking becomes *worry.* "What if my son doesn't adjust well to preschool?" "What if I can't handle the increased responsibilities my new job will demand?" Worry is the mental condition in which we are preoccupied with a problem, having repetitive and distressing thoughts that intensify sensations of anxiety.

Panic is a state of terror without a good reason for it: intense physical arousal and terrified thoughts of dying, going crazy, or losing control.

This book will help you better manage these troublesome states of mind. Let's now take a closer look at anxiety.

Anxiety is a very real medical issue with symptoms that are:

- Emotional (dread, fearing panic, fearing social situations, etc.)
- Physical (racing heart, dizziness, shortness of breath, lump in the throat, tingling, etc.)
- Mental (worrying, preoccupation with fear, fear of dying or going crazy, etc.)

There is a critical difference between panic and acute anxiety. Many people think they "panic all day," but in the clinical sense, a true panic attack is quite brief—only minutes in duration. That said, the aftermath of a panic attack can last for hours, leaving a person tired, weak, and nauseated, with a "gut feeling" that something is wrong. We'll look more closely at panic attacks in Part II.

Acute anxiety is an intense feeling of dread or doom, but it doesn't have the intense, heart-pounding physical arousal that goes with panic. It is a sense of anticipation of trouble. You might have this sensation if you receive a phone call saying your child is injured at school, or if your parent goes to the hospital with chest pain, or if your spouse says, "We have to talk," with no indication of what that talk will be about. In these situations, you feel intensely worried. Your heart rate rises a little, you feel a bit sick, and you can think of nothing but whether things will be okay. That heightened negative mental and physical arousal continues until you know things are okay or have a sense that you can do something to deal with the situation. This acutely anxious feeling can go on for hours.

Another important distinction is the difference between *feelings* of panic or anxiety and anxiety *disorders*. Anyone can experience feelings of panic or anxiety, and the presence of such feelings doesn't necessarily mean you have an anxiety *disorder*. It's only when you become preoccupied with avoiding feelings of panic and anxiety—to the point that you begin changing your life—that you are considered to have an anxiety disorder.

There are several different kinds of anxiety disorders:

- Panic disorder
- Generalized anxiety disorder
- Social anxiety disorder
- Agoraphobia
- Specific phobia

- Post-traumatic stress disorder (PTSD)
- Obsessive-compulsive disorder (OCD)

We'll look at each of these more closely later in the chapter.

Different kinds of anxiety have different causes, and anxiety may worsen in common life situations. Some causes are:

- A genetic predisposition to feeling anxiety when under stress
- Experiencing anxiety as extremely unpleasant and something that must be avoided at all costs
- Exceptional or ongoing (chronic) stress
- Trauma in the recent or distant past
- Other diverse medical, biological, or life situations

Certain kinds of medical conditions can cause symptoms identical to those of anxiety, so before you assume you suffer from anxiety, see a physician for a checkup to rule out these medical conditions. Also, many medications can create the side effect of anxiety. Although it's uncommon, even medications your physician might prescribe to calm you down can have the unintended effect of raising anxiety. Common medical causes of anxiety-like symptoms include:

- Heart conditions
- Thyroid problems
- Blood sugar imbalances (diabetes or hypoglycemia)
- Hormone changes, including those that may accompany contraceptive methods
- Stimulating drugs, such as steroids or those prescribed for asthma
- Medication side effects or adverse reactions

Ironically, far too often people with anxiety consult their physician when they do *not* have a medical condition causing their anxiety symptoms. The physical sensations of anxiety lead them to believe that their problems *must* be physical because they are felt in the body. Anxiety does have physical symptoms and implications, but it doesn't necessarily stem from a disease or medical condition.

It is no surprise that anxiety has different causes and comes in different forms. Some people suffer from panic attacks that come out of the blue; others feel consumed by worry on a nearly constant basis. It is also no surprise that some people have confusing combinations of anxiety symptoms. Some wonder if their anxiety is normal or might actually be a disorder. Especially when life events are anxiety-provoking, it can be hard to know if your anxiety is a normal reaction or has become a problem that needs attention.

Regardless of the origin of your symptoms, once you feel anxiety, you will benefit from the techniques in this workbook. The following sections will help you identify what kind of anxiety you suffer from.

PANIC DISORDER

Panic attacks are bouts of sudden, intense feelings (physical sensations and emotions) of fear or terror that last 11 to 13 minutes. They typically leave you feeling weak, exhausted, and scared for minutes or even hours after the attack subsides.

Have You Suffered a Panic Attack?

Check off your symptoms in the following list. During the attack, did you experience:

☑ A rapid heart rate
☑ Rapid, shallow breathing
☑ Nausea
☑ Sweating
☐ An urge to urinate or diarrhea
☑ Tightness or pain in your chest
☑ The feeling that you couldn't breathe or couldn't catch your breath
☐ A lump in your throat or choking sensation
☑ Shaking/trembling
☑ Dizziness
☐ Feelings of unreality
☑ The belief that you were dying, going crazy, or about to lose control

If you felt five or more of these symptoms, you probably suffered a panic attack.

It's possible to experience panic attacks without suffering from panic *disorder*. Panic attacks are unpleasant. They are inconvenient. You are not happy to have them. But in and of themselves, they are not a mental health disorder. It is rather *worrying about* having panic attacks and *changing your life* to avoid them that indicates panic disorder.

Do You Have Panic Disorder?

If you have experienced at least one panic attack, check which of the following changes you have made. Have you:

- ☐ Worried about having panic attacks so much that you were distracted from work or social exchanges
- ☐ Stopped attending activities you previously enjoyed
- ☒ Limited driving to roads on which you feel safe from panic
- ☒ Avoided transportation that you think you might panic on and not be able to leave at will (e.g., a subway, bus, plane, boat, ferry)
- ☐ Avoided social situations where you fear you might panic (e.g., parties, stadiums)
- ☐ Stayed out of theaters, restaurants, or public meeting places for fear you will panic
- ☐ Started paying attention to exits and ways to escape a location
- ☐ Gone to the emergency room more than once to make sure you were not having a heart attack
- ☐ Avoided going into classrooms with too few or too many other students
- ☐ Stayed home from school for fear of having an attack
- ☐ Stopped shopping in stores when there are people who might observe you panicking (e.g., started grocery shopping late at night)
- ☐ Stopped exercising because you feared that rapid heart rate or respiration would trigger a panic attack
- ☒ Insisted that a family member or friend accompany you for travel, even for short distances, or accompany you into retail stores

How many did you check? If you checked:

1 = You don't have panic disorder yet, but don't make this behavior a habit! Know that you can control panic better than you can control situations or people.

2 = You are starting to change your behavior to accommodate panic. Ask yourself if giving up activities or making life more complicated is *really* better than managing panic.

3 = You may have panic disorder. You are certainly afraid of feeling afraid! Although this doesn't guarantee that you have the disorder, you are definitely changing your life to avoid panic attacks.

4 or more = Avoiding panic is controlling your life. You will benefit from learning how to stop panic attacks and may want some guidance to help you begin doing things you've been avoiding.

The problem with avoiding panic attacks is that it works! But if you change your life to avoid panic, you give up your control and hand it over to the panic.

AGORAPHOBIA

Some people develop agoraphobia (fear of public places) as a result of avoiding panic attacks. For them, the avoidance offers so much relief that the subsequent loss of social engagement seems inconsequential. Losing out on fun and time with others seems a small price to pay for not feeling afraid (panicking). Some people with agoraphobia are so limited that they rarely leave their homes, whereas others go out but severely curtail where they go and with whom (e.g., they will not cross a bridge or go into a stadium). Inability to escape is a major concern. The range of choices of where you can go and whom you can go with narrows until leaving the house requires thought, as shown in Figure 1.1.

This book does not address agoraphobia directly. If the agoraphobia started with panic, then managing panic successfully should help you undo the fear of going out. If your agoraphobia did not begin with panic, there are probably complicating factors that require psychotherapy.

GENERALIZED ANXIETY

Whereas those with panic disorder have a specific, single fear (fearing a panic attack), people with generalized anxiety disorder worry constantly about a wide variety of things. These things may change over time, but the condition of worry remains constant.

The serious impairment to life that generalized anxiety engenders is grossly underestimated. The gnawing feeling in your gut, the preoccupation and loss of attention, the sense of doom and misery, and the physical agitation all combine to create major impediments to participating in life. Loss of pleasure and constant worry undermine sleep as well as daytime activities so that you have no respite even during the night.

You may wonder if your worry is severe enough to be considered a disorder. Figure 1.2 lists the differences between "normal" worry and excessive worry.

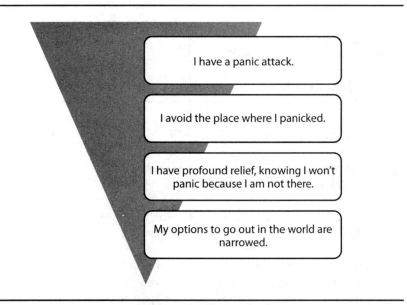

Figure 1.1 Agoraphobia Narrows Choices

Do You Have Generalized Anxiety?

If the items in the "excessive worry" column in Figure 1.2 seem to pertain to you, read the following list and check off the questions to which you can answer yes.

☐ I worry a lot on most days, and this has been going on for six months or more.

☐ I ruin whole days or good events by worrying, and my worries are often unreasonable, even though they're about normal things like work, school performance, physical health, and friendships.

☐ No matter how hard I try, I can't seem to stop the worry.

If you answered "yes" to these three questions, your anxiety is greater than normal and you may have generalized anxiety disorder.

Certain physical conditions accompany generalized anxiety. They are the result of the underlying brain chemistry that creates worry and of the worry itself, which produces tension.

NORMAL WORRY *Situation-specific, resolves with resolution of the situation*	GENERALIZED ANXIETY WORRY *Excessive time consumed, resolved worries are quickly replaced with new worries*
I am worried about my daughter being safe on a mountain-climbing expedition.	Every time my daughter leaves the house, I worry that she won't return safely.
I worry about the safety of driving in bad weather and am very cautious on the road.	I feel intensely worried about the weather and will not drive if rain is predicted.
I worry about how I will pay a bill that is unexpected, and I try to figure it out.	I worry every day about how I would manage financially if I lost my job.
When my kids have a physical symptom like a fever, I worry about whether it will get too high and I watch them carefully.	I feel frantic with worry whenever my children have a fever or other physical symptom and am afraid they will die.
I am worried before I take a test about how hard it will be and if I will get a passing grade.	I worry about not being smart enough and am constantly comparing my grades to those of my friends.
I worry about my spouse's drug relapse damaging our relationship permanently.	Whenever I am in a relationship I worry about when it will end.
I want my children to be safe, so I research whether chemicals I use around the house could be toxic if they are ingested.	I am constantly worried about whether my children will be harmed by environmental toxins and I am always online searching for hazards I may not be aware of.
I sometimes worry if I have an unusual physical symptom, and I check it out with a doctor if the symptom does not go away in a reasonable time.	I research all my symptoms online, no matter how minor they are, to be sure I don't have a serious disease.

Figure 1.2 Normal Worry Versus Excessive Worry

Do You Have Physical Symptoms of Generalized Anxiety?

Check the box below if you experience:

- ☑ Muscle tension, such as TMJ (temporomandibular joint disorder) or aching in your neck or back
- ☑ Headaches
- ☐ Irritable bowel syndrome (aggravated by tension)
- ☑ Irritability
- ☑ Restless sleep or fatigue on awakening
- ☑ Physical jumpiness

If you have three or more of these symptoms, pay careful attention to Technique #1 about changing your intake and Technique #4 on rest and relaxation. And watch for the feelings of depression that follow prolonged worry and anxiety. There is a big overlap between depression and generalized anxiety, and once you become depressed, your energy for overcoming the anxiety will be seriously depleted. You may need psychotherapy to help you work on these disorders.

SOCIAL ANXIETY DISORDER

People who are shy are mildly familiar with the symptoms of social anxiety. You may not want to be the center of attention or perform in public. There is nothing wrong with being shy, and most shy people have satisfying lives without their shyness getting in the way of accomplishments. But when you have social anxiety, there are big impairments in fulfilling your potential because you avoid challenging experiences that could help you grow and develop your abilities. Social anxiety may be something you're born with, and it gets worse for most people who don't get good help. It can be seen in childhood, adolescence, or adulthood. Most people with social anxiety experience their anxiety as too uncomfortable to tolerate. They are sensitive to the very feeling of anxiety and try to avoid feeling it.

There are three categories of common symptoms for social anxiety, which involve avoiding whatever it is that might make you feel uncomfortable. These have to do with feeling uncomfortable being observed, anticipating being judged for inevitable social gaffes, or having mistaken beliefs.

Do You Have Social Anxiety?

What is your score in these three categories? The typical ways that people fear being observed are varied. Check statements that apply to you.

Do you fear being observed while:

☐ Eating in restaurant
☐ Signing a check or credit card receipt
☐ Answering a question at school
☐ Speaking up at a business meeting
☐ Leaving your seat during a movie or theater performance

People with social anxiety also fear being judged. Do you fear that in social situations you will:

☐ Not be able to think of interesting things to say
☐ Not be likable
☐ Blush or be silent when meeting new people
☐ Reveal some social inadequacy, such as wearing the wrong clothes, or not know a "social grace," such as which fork to use at a set table
☐ Embarrass yourself by saying the wrong thing

If you have social anxiety, you are likely to:

☐ Assume others know the right way to do things
☐ Assume you are the only one who doesn't know the right answers or who has ever made a mistake learning something new
☐ Believe that you will be rejected in new situations
☐ Assume that other people are watching you when you are in public
☐ Believe that feeling humiliated is inevitable and you won't be able to get over it

Of the 15 items above, how many did you check? If you checked:

2 or fewer = You do not have social anxiety disorder. Everyone feels these things from time to time.
3 = You are probably holding back from situations.
4 or more = You are too worried about your social acceptability and may be suffering from social anxiety. The techniques in this book will help you desensitize yourself and unlearn fear.

> **Is Social Anxiety Interfering With Your Life?**
>
> Your social anxieties are interfering with your life if you avoid *any* of the following:
>
> ☐ Going into new situations (a new club, schoolroom, activity)
> ☐ Auditioning or interviewing for positions you are qualified to hold
> ☐ Speaking up at a meeting
> ☐ Speaking up in a classroom
> ☐ Talking to supervisors about work-related issues
> ☐ Talking to people you don't know
> ☐ Attending gatherings of people, even to advance your career or celebrate an event

Performance anxiety is a form of social anxiety. This is when you have one specific social situation that gives you anxiety—such as singing in public, giving a speech, auditioning, or standing up in a classroom. Your anxiety may be intense enough to make you avoid that situation at all costs, but it is restricted to that one kind of circumstance. There are many treatments—such as energy therapies and eye movement desensitization and reprocessing (EMDR)—that can help you overcome performance anxiety. See the Resources section at the end of the book.

SPECIFIC PHOBIA

A phobia is a fear of a specific thing, such as snakes, spiders, or insects. Many people suffer from phobias, which usually cause only minor interference with life. However, some specific phobias—like fear of the dark, driving over a bridge, or claustrophobia—can be debilitating because they interfere with many life situations.

Some phobias don't seem related to any specific event that started the fear. These can usually be treated fairly easily with any of several desensitization methods. When the phobia is the outcome of a traumatic experience, the right treatment depends on the type of event and the kinds of repercussions still present in your life.

POST-TRAUMATIC STRESS DISORDER

Over the past decade, as combat veterans have struggled to reintegrate into civilian life, post-traumatic stress disorder (PTSD) has received a lot of well-deserved attention in the press. However, it's not only combat veterans who develop PTSD. This serious condition may affect you as the result of any experience:

- That threatened your life or the life of someone else in your presence
- That created a sense of terror
- In which you were not in control, such as a natural disaster, war, or crime

When people of any age have had such an experience, they may begin to experience serious symptoms that disrupt their lives and well-being. They may have nightmares or flashbacks in which they reexperience all or part of the trauma. They may become depressed or anxious, have trouble concentrating or sleeping, and become easily agitated or even angry and rageful. These symptoms usually appear about a month after the event, but sometimes they don't occur for many months or even years.

Not everyone gets PTSD as a result of such experiences, because even after such an acute experience of terror, you may have emotional and practical resources and even the right kind of brain function that makes you resilient enough to recover either quickly or over time. People who undergo training to face frightening or disastrous situations, such as firefighters, emergency room workers, and relief workers, have preparation that helps with the emotional arousal of such frightening events, so they may not have the stress response to the traumatic event that a novice might, but even they may develop PTSD when too many experiences or a particularly awful experience rocks their ability to handle it.

Recent research has indicated that combat veterans who are victims of blasts from explosive devices may have physical damage to the brain causing emotional symptoms that are more complicated than PTSD without brain damage, and they will need specialized evaluation and medical interventions. (If you are interested in researching this, start with the work of Dr. Rajendra Morey at Duke University or Dr. Daniel Perl at the Uniformed Services University of the Health Sciences at Bethesda, MD, or look for blast injury information on the website for the Center for Disease Control and Prevention, www.cdc.gov) The fortunate news is that to recover from the depression, anxiety, and other PTSD symptoms, a person suffering from blast injuries can utilize all the standard psychological PTSD treatments.

Although all the techniques discussed in this book will help manage the symptoms of anxiety accompanying PTSD, they won't resolve the traumatic experience; that will require trauma treatment. Several types have been found to be very effective, including EMDR, rapid resolution therapy (RRT), brainspotting, energy "tapping" by various names, and many other useful approaches. If you suffer from PTSD or suspect that you do, consult a therapist. Help is available!

OBSESSIVE-COMPULSIVE DISORDER

Unlike the other anxiety disorders, obsessive-compulsive disorder (OCD) is not caused by life events. You can be taught to worry too much or be too cautious, but you can't be taught to be a compulsive hand-washer, checker, or hoarder. OCD is a neurobiological problem that people are born with, though it may not emerge until adolescence or adulthood. Why it emerges at a certain age is not well understood, but some OCD may be triggered by strep infections that are insufficiently treated.

Signs of OCD include unreasonable, obsessive worries and fears. These obsessive thoughts may cause a person to develop ritualistic behaviors ("compulsions") to try to relieve the anxiety caused by the obsessive thought. Some compulsions, like repeated hand-washing, are obvious, but others are much more subtle, such as touching a talisman or leaving the house on the same foot every time you walk out.

People with OCD are often stricken with uncertainty about whether they have completed a certain task, and this sense of incompleteness leads them to do the behavior over and over. Some obsessions do not include rituals but involve counting, organizing in the mind, or scrupulously reciting prayers. Adults may not be able to control their behavior but know their obsessions and compulsions are unrealistic. Children are often unaware that their ideas are unrealistic and may not voluntarily bring them to your attention.

The techniques in this book that involve calming your physiology will help you if you have OCD, but the cognitive techniques are not well suited to treatment of the disorder. Go to the International Obsessive-Compulsive Foundation website (see the Resources section) for signs, symptoms, and ideas for treatment.

COEXISTING CONDITIONS

Some common mental health conditions can cause anxiety or intensify anxiety, and they confuse the picture as to whether a discrete anxiety disorder exists. Three in particular should be mentioned: attention-deficit disorder, with or without hyper-activity (ADD, ADHD); high-functioning autism spectrum disorder (ASD); and addiction, especially alcoholism.

Attention-Deficit Hyperactivity Disorder (ADHD)

People who have ADHD often feel anxious about the way their problems with attention interfere with remembering, following through, and completing work assignments or schoolwork. Children who have academic difficulties are screened for ADHD and other learning disabilities (LD), but not all people with ADHD do poorly academically and, thus, do not come to the attention of the school for LD screening. Their ADHD may go unrecognized for a long time, especially if they don't show hyperactivity. Those with ADHD may suffer considerable, legitimate worry about whether they have taken care of necessary tasks or noticed everything they should notice. Because they often have trouble organizing, finding workable methods to help track responsibilities is a challenge. They are prone to time-gobbling accidents, such as spilling, breaking, or losing things. Fearing that one has made mistakes is not an unreasonable thing to do, but the worry can grow to uncontrollable proportions. The best remedy for anxiety about the real problems created by ADD is actively treating the disorder with strategies and medication when appropriate.

Do You Need an ADD/ADHD Evaluation?

Even if you were not diagnosed with ADHD in childhood, it may be a good idea to be screened if you begin to experience anxiety and have some of the indicators in the following lists (the first is for adolescents; the second is for adults). In people who have done well academically, the appearance of intense anxiety during or immedi-ately following life transitions warrants careful attention.

Do You Have ADD?

Are you an adolescent who has done well in school (at least until now) and is currently:

☐ Applying for college and feeling overwhelmed by the choices of where to go

☐ Applying for college but avoiding the confusing demands of the applications (essays, collecting documents and recommendations, submitting resumes, or answering questions)

☐ Taking AP classes and feeling overwhelmed by the assignments or expectations (you may be feeling test anxiety for the first time)

☐ Doing a new responsibility—such as editing the yearbook, participating in the student council, or being a team captain or an officer in a school organization—and feeling panicked about the duties

☐ Doing part-time work in addition to school and feeling overwhelmed about keeping the schedule straight and getting all your work done

Adolescents who checked any of the above questions should get an ADHD screening.

In their online newsletter, *Harvard Health Publications* stated:

> "The profile of an adult with ADHD can vary from that of a child. Most experts agree that pure hyperactive behavior usually diminishes with maturity. Adults usually have problems with time management, self-control, planning for the future, and being able to persist toward goals." (www.health.harvard.edu/press_releases/adult_adhd_treatment)

In my clinical experience, when people with ADHD are intelligent and do well academically, they don't come to the attention of the school as having learning problems. But they may suffer intense anxiety about making mistakes, which they legitimately make but can't figure out how to avoid. They may not cross this threshold until the responsibility they take on exceeds whatever strategies they developed to manage the ADHD without realizing they were managing it. Then they worry about their competency or ability to succeed. If you are not achieving what you know you are capable of, feeling anxiety about competency even though you are stably employed, or having difficulty keeping your home organized despite making an effort, you might want to consider whether ADHD may be playing a role in this.

Do You Have ADHD?

Are you an adult who has become exceedingly anxious (panicky, worried, or both) and has also:

- ☐ Historically been disorganized at work and relied on colleagues or assistants to get the organization done
- ☐ Failed to complete tasks, regardless of whether you enjoy the work
- ☐ Been hyperfocused on certain things, like video games, that stimulate you
- ☐ Avoided jobs that require you to complete paperwork or organize environments
- ☐ Avoided reading, especially texts and manuals, and preferred to learn new information by doing the task
- ☐ Done very well in your work until you got promoted and now feel incompetent or worried about losing your job
- ☐ Recently become a parent and begun to feel as if everything is overwhelming and too much to keep track of, despite previously doing very well in your job and successfully managing home life
- ☐ Found yourself, after a change in work or home duties, being suddenly forgetful and missing appointments, deadlines, or conference calls that you previously might have managed
- ☐ Saying way too much and then wishing you had more restraint

If you checked any two of the criteria above, you should take a screening test for ADHD and seek ADHD treatment in addition to anxiety management.

Parents of adolescents often assume their teen's anxiety is related to separation from home to attend college or to taking classes that are too difficult, and they want the adolescent to learn anxiety/stress management and homework strategies. In these cases, anxiety management requires managing ADHD and then learning to calm the physiology and manage worry.

If you think you may have ADHD, see www.add.org for a host of reliable resources for screening and treatment. Also check out the Harvard Medical School screening tool for adult attention-deficit disorder: https://hcp.med.harvard.edu/ncs/ftpdir/adhd/18Q_ASRS_English.pdf.

High-Functioning ASD

According to the Centers for Disease Control and Prevention, approximately 1 in 68 children in the United States have symptoms that place them on the autism disorder spectrum. This disorder, which affects the development of language and social skills, may cause impairments that are mild and hard to detect or may severely impair normal development. In high-functioning individuals, ASD symptoms can be mistaken for social anxiety. Those symptoms may include:

- Sensitivity to environmental stimulation
- Social awkwardness and lack of responsiveness to emotional signals from others
- Body language or vocalization that is "off"—not exactly matching the words or social circumstance
- Indirect or very brief eye contact
- Intense, narrow interests
- Physical clumsiness
- Behavior seen by peers as "odd"

The key to differentiating high-functioning ASD from social anxiety lies in examining the individual's interest in and ability to relate to others. Socially anxious children and young adults may be very interested in friendships and able to interact but uncertain or embarrassed about their lack of social experience or shyness. Although they prefer one-on-one interactions or small groups, they can learn to participate with groups in activities they enjoy, such as sports. They clearly understand social signals although they may be overreactive to negative signals. The child with high-functioning ASD, on the other hand, may want to interact with others but have trouble reading social signals correctly. These children need specific instruction about how to recognize social signals and how to show socially appropriate responses.

A major challenge for people with high-functioning ASD is their difficulty with changing: changing the topic of discussion, changing the activity, changing their location, or changing any routine. For them, safety is in knowing what to expect and how to react, so in new situations they may feel intense anxiety; thus, they make efforts to avoid new and unfamiliar circumstances. People with social anxiety may also avoid what is new or unfamiliar but for a different reason: they do not want to be observed making mistakes or looking embarrassed, which could result in being rejected by others. They would be happy to learn new things if they were not being observed while doing so. And whereas people with high-functioning ASD have difficulty identifying what others think, feel, or are interested in, socially anxious people are overly tuned in to others, overestimating the degree of disapproval they might experience.

Because high-functioning ASD makes forming successful connections with others difficult, young people with the disorder may develop anxiety or depression. However, interventions to help children develop communication and social skills are effective at improving a child's ability to thrive, and the earlier those interventions can be started, the more effective they are at improving development in those areas.

It is suggested by the American Academy of Pediatrics (www.aap.org) that all children get screened for the autism spectrum at 18 months of age. A useful screening tool is the M-CHAT-R/F , which can be found at www.mchatscreen.com.

Addiction

Many people with anxiety turn to alcohol to calm themselves, which can lead to alcohol abuse or addiction. Another issue is how to recognize and treat anxiety disorder if you are an alcoholic in recovery. Anxiety can lead to relapse if you are not managing your anxiety symptoms.

If you are in recovery from alcohol addiction, managing your anxiety may require more than your addiction treatment program or 12-step self-help program (both of which I believe in!) can provide. Do not regard it as a treatment failure if you need more strategies than addiction recovery to deal with anxiety. Your anxiety may have predated the addiction, even if you didn't recognize it. But once anxiety is present, it needs to be managed.

The issue of addiction is too big to address here except in the broadest strokes. Here are some bullet points:

- Stimulant abuse can trigger anxiety that persists into recovery.
- You may develop addiction if you use marijuana, alcohol, food, or the Internet to handle anxiety or social fears.
- Alcohol causes a rebound to more intense anxiety. If you slip during recovery, the subsequent anxiety may be due to more than just your worries about the relapse.
- Addiction may both calm anxiety and *cause* it as financial, interpersonal, health, and legal issues surrounding addiction begin to mount.

If you are in recovery, don't underestimate the power of anxiety to interfere with your progress. Seek help to manage your anxiety rather than risking relapse. For those of you with anxiety who are abusing substances or behaviors, anxiety treatment may be the start of recovery.

RESOURCES

The Resources section at the end of this book lists many websites and books that can provide more information on anxiety and related problems. If you have questions about your symptoms and wonder whether you might have anxiety, there are several excellent self-tests on the website of the Anxiety Disorder Association of America (www.adaa.org). You should be aware that many web resources offer free self-tests, but most also want to sell you a program for self-help that may or may not be useful. The advent of web-based learning is putting many excellent tools out online for people with limited access to therapists who are skilled in treating anxiety. If you have social anxiety, you may think an online program is ideal, but I urge you to consider how valuable a face-to-face relationship with a therapist would be to developing your social confidence. A good evaluation by a skilled professional should be the next step after self-testing on the Internet.

Anxiety disorders can be treated by a wide range of mental health professionals, most typically psychologists, clinical social workers, and counselors. Although all psychiatrists and most primary care physicians will prescribe medication for anxiety, they don't usually offer therapy to teach you techniques that control anxiety symptoms. That's where therapists come in.

Choosing a Therapist

If you seek help from a therapist, which is often a good idea, it's best to find someone who is oriented to helping you diminish symptoms of anxiety as well as working through underlying psychological issues. Finding the right therapist is not always easy, as many competent therapists with good credentials don't always practice the pragmatic style of thought and behavior management that works best with anxiety symptoms. There are several ways to begin a search for a therapist. Ask your doctor for a referral or look on the Anxiety Disorder Association of America's website (www.adaa.org) for a list of therapists in your area who belong to the association. Therapists who specialize in trauma treatment are also likely to have experience in treating anxiety. EMDR is a form of therapy that uses a technique called "dual-attention stimulus" (such as alternate hand-tapping) to help resolve symptoms resulting from disturbing, unresolved life experiences. Visit the EMDR International Association website (www.emdria.org) for a list of therapists who are trained in that method in your area. Many therapists list their interests and specialties on the websites for their professional organizations or on sites like Psychology Today.

When you find a therapist in your area, ask to speak to that person before you schedule an appointment. Don't hesitate to ask questions about the therapist's training, his or her style of working, and relevant details about the therapy sessions (times, cost, etc.). These questions don't require long answers or explanations, and a therapist who treats anxiety well will be able to respond quickly to them.

Questions to Ask

Following are some questions and guidelines to use when seeking a therapist to treat your anxiety.

- Ask, "What training and experience do you have in treating anxiety?" You might also ask some of these questions:
  - "What is your therapy approach to anxiety?" (Ask about the type of anxiety you have.)
  - "What kinds of cognitive techniques do you use?"
  - "Do you give 'homework' assignments?"
  - "What methods might you recommend for panic attacks?"
- Ask, "What do you believe about the need to get rid of underlying causes of anxiety in order to get rid of symptoms?" Ideally, you will get an answer that suggests:
  - Symptom management may be possible without long-term work, *and*
  - If anxiety is caused by unresolved issues (such as a previous trauma), it will come back unless the person deals with those issues.
- Ask, "How frequently will you expect to see me, and how long does one session last?"
- Ask, "Do you include family members in treatment?"
  - If seeking help for a child, parents must be included.
  - It is a good idea for a spouse or partner to hear about the biological nature of anxiety and to learn from the therapist how to respond to the complaints of anxiety that come up at home.
- Ask, "What is your fee schedule?"
  - Ask for details about insurance coverage, sliding fees, and so on.
  - Ask about community resources for special financial circumstances.

Remember, if a therapist is skilled in treating anxiety, his or her answers to these questions should be clear and direct. Any therapist who is vague or reluctant to answer your questions may not have the skills you need to improve your anxiety rapidly.

The 10 Best-Ever Anxiety Management Techniques Workbook

Treatment Options

There are three prongs involved in anxiety treatment: techniques that focus on the body, techniques that focus on the mind (cognition), and techniques that focus on behavior. Some types of techniques are better than others for certain kinds of anxiety—for example, those that focus on the body are best for panic disorder—but, generally speaking, a combination of all three types is most effective.

The following treatment options are the most commonly used for anxiety.

Relaxation Techniques

Relaxation techniques, such as diaphragmatic breathing and progressive muscle relaxation, help to diminish physical symptoms of anxiety, and you can learn and practice these techniques on your own. Relaxation and other techniques that target physical symptoms are described in Chapters 3 through 6 of this book, and the Resources section will direct you to various options you can learn from or follow along with over the Internet.

Cognitive-Behavioral Therapy

Cognitive-behavioral therapy (CBT) identifies anxious patterns of both thought and behavior that keep unwanted symptoms in place. Using CBT methods learned in therapy sessions, people can begin to cope with anxiety-producing situations and control thoughts and behaviors that keep anxiety in place or harm them socially and emotionally. Individuals are involved at all times in planning and practicing techniques for their recovery.

Chapters 7 through 9 of this book offer techniques that focus on the mind, and Chapters 10 through 12 include techniques that target behavior. You can learn and use these techniques on your own, but they may be more effective if you also seek the help of a therapist trained in CBT.

Medication

Medication is often used in conjunction with psychotherapy. It is often not necessary but may be very helpful. Typical medication choices for anxiety reduction include selective serotonin reuptake inhibitors (SSRIs, which are often confusingly called "antidepressants") and limited use of benzodiazepines.

A FINAL WORD

Anxiety disorders are treatable. Treatment varies with the type of anxiety you have and whether you are experiencing more than one kind of anxiety. Improvement in physical symptoms, such as panic, may occur fairly quickly (perhaps within a few months), whereas diminishing persistent worry may take longer. Treatment is always geared to individual situations: what type of anxiety you have, how long the condition has lasted, what kinds of life situations affect you, and so on. No single plan works for everyone.

The goal of this workbook is to help all anxiety sufferers, regardless of whether you are also getting help from a professional. If you have success using the techniques presented here without the help of a professional guide, good for you! But if you still find yourself struggling after trying the techniques, don't give up. It is likely that all you need is the guidance of a psychotherapist to make these 10 best-ever anxiety management techniques work for you.

TWO

Assess Your Stress

Many people talk about being "stressed out" and "feeling stressed." Most of us know what the general expression implies. However, stress is a physical and emotional state that has diverse symptoms, and it can create big problems if you don't recognize it and respond to it well. It can create or magnify anxiety and deplete your resources to deal with it.

Before we look at stress specifically, you should have a bit of knowledge about brain science. You don't need to know brain science to be able to effectively use the techniques in this book, but a little understanding may help you apply them. The following section covers the basics; for a more in-depth discussion of brain science, see my books *The 10 Best-Ever Anxiety Management Techniques* and *The Anxious Brain*.

BRAIN BASICS

All of our emotional reactions are experienced physically and mentally. Your brain sets those reactions in motion when you experience stimulation from the world around you or from inside of yourself or when your thoughts prompt emotion. Although all the parts of your brain should work smoothly in concert with each other, certain parts of your brain have specific functions. Deep in the center of the brain, you have a system that recognizes and reacts to signals from the world around you as well as to your internal world. It is called the limbic system. Thinking does not occur in this part of the brain. Rather, the structures of the limbic system immediately note the importance and quality of those signals without putting any words to the situation. A smile or a frown, a siren or a chime (any kind of signal creates an emotional tone)—is it safe or not safe? important or not important? You will immediately have a physical change, faster than you can think, based on how this system assesses the signal.

Another part of your brain—the one you consciously think with—is slower to respond (although it still responds pretty darned fast!), and what you think about the signal is colored by the way your body is responding. In this front-and-center part of the brain, you gather the information together, think things over, and make decisions about whether the emotional response makes sense or should be changed somehow. An example of this might be the process of getting mad but cooling off when you realize the other person didn't mean to insult you, or feeling nervous about meeting someone new but then thinking the person is really quite friendly and consequently feeling less nervous.

All of those processes are conducted by electrical signals and chemical messengers (neurotransmitters) that carry specific kinds of messages depending on where in the brain they are active. Medications affect the chemical messages, but the good news—and the reason the techniques in this workbook will work—is that you can deliberately change the message by using the "thinking" part of your brain. Ultimately, that will change the ways the messengers work, promoting better functioning of your brain.

Now let's look at how stress affects the brain and body.

WHAT'S HAPPENING WHEN YOU'RE STRESSED?

Your body reacts to challenges via two physiological systems: the "fight-or-flight" response and the stress response. Both responses are active when you experience a stressful event. You've probably heard of fight-or-flight. This is the automatic physical response that occurs when you get worked up emotionally, mentally, or physically. If you have to run to catch a bus, you don't *decide* to have increased respiration or a faster heartbeat. This automatic function works without your conscious thought. Your nervous system increases your heart rate, blood pressure, and respiration; changes your blood flow; and generally makes sure you are ready to move physically. Whether you are climbing stairs (you need more energy *now*) or listening to a parent yelling (a possible threat indicating that you *might* need to move fast), this system goes to work. It's called the "fight-or-flight" response because it prepares you to do just that—run away from danger or protect yourself from it. If you need to make a *big* response to a challenge, your body has to be ready.

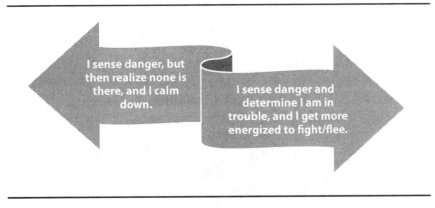

Figure 2.1 Thinking Controls Automatic Fight or Flight

How does this automatic system get turned on? It's triggered by the fast-acting part of the limbic system called the amygdala, which is always alert and scanning for danger. If it notices anything in the world around you that is a potential risk to your safety, your body responds immediately so you are ready to act, even before you have time to think. For example, if a siren goes off, you immediately have a burst of "fight-or-flight" in case you must run to get out of there. Once you have time to think and you decide there is no need to worry or act, this arousal settles back down. If your thinking brain says there is danger, however, the arousal remains or intensifies. Figure 2.1 illustrates this.

FIGHT-OR-FLIGHT AND ANXIETY

If you have panic or anxiety, it may start with a physical feeling—even though no real danger exists. Your brain doesn't like it when you have a physical sensation without an observable reason, so it decides, "If I feel this bad, there must be something wrong!" Your helpful brain starts to look around for a reason you're having a racing heart or shallow breathing, and it's usually good at tricking itself into thinking it's found one. For example, if you have that kind of panicky sensation while you're entering your first big lecture in college, or driving on the highway in heavy traffic, or meeting new colleagues for the first time, your brain might decide that what you were doing *caused* the burst of fight-or-flight energy. It might not notice it was the other way around—the feeling preceded the activity and maybe was

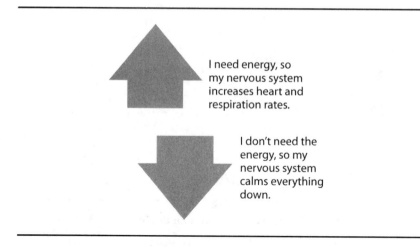

I need energy, so my nervous system increases heart and respiration rates.

I don't need the energy, so my nervous system calms everything down.

Figure 2.2 Your Body Is Either Getting Aroused or Calming Down

unrelated to it. But once it decides that the activity caused the panic, you might be inclined to avoid that situation in the future in an attempt to avoid feeling bad.

The good news about the arousal response is that you can't become aroused and calm down at the same time: you are either working up to fight-or-flight or calming it down, as depicted in Figure 2.2. This is the physical reality that underlies control of panic. You can use the calming system to decrease all the negative symptoms of a panic attack.

If you feel physical energy—such as anticipation of fun, sexual excitement, or the outcome of physical exercise—and you interpret that energy as a good thing, you won't be disturbed. Your brain knows something good is the cause. But when that nonthinking alarm goes off—saying, "Look out!"—you will go on the alert, and your heart rate will increase. If it is mild, you might be able to ignore it, but if you are in danger and you know you are, you will have a sudden, intense arousal of the fight-or-flight system. That is appropriate to help you respond to the danger and get to safety. The outcome is depicted in Figure 2.3.

When this sudden acceleration happens *in the absence of* real danger, it's called a panic attack. Your heart can go up to 200 beats a minute and your breath can get short and shallow, even panting. Your nervous system gives you a jolt of adrenaline so that you will have the readiness to fight hard or run fast. It is mentally disconcerting to be that aroused without knowing the reason, and you may fear that you are dying, going crazy, or losing control when you have a panic attack. The feeling of dying is so real that many people rush to the hospital, sure they are having a heart attack.

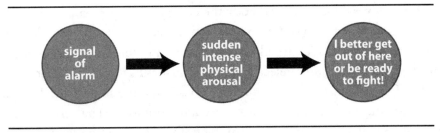

Figure 2.3 Fight or Flight Arousal Prepares You for Action

When a panic attack is over, a person can be left feeling jangled and exhausted. Even though the average panic attack peaks after only 11 to 13 minutes, the aftermath can last for hours. One particularly disturbing outcome of a panic attack is that you may have a persistent sensation that something bad is happening or will happen. This feeling may last for hours and can be hard to shake off. One of my clients, Glenda, gave an excellent example of this. She was driving on a snowy day when her car was hit by another car skidding on the slippery road. She felt a jolt of shock and panicked for a few minutes until she realized there was no injury and her car was drivable despite noticeable rear-end damage. Later that evening, though, she began to feel sick. Her heart rate was only slightly elevated and her breathing was normal, but she couldn't shake the feeling that something was wrong. So she began to think that the sick-with-worry sensation was present because she had neglected to make a police report and only took the other driver's insurance information. Then she spent the night trying to figure out what would happen. She imagined that failure to call the police would result in an insurance denial of the claim, and her husband would be furious, and it would cost more money than she could afford, and so on and so on until she was emotionally tied in knots. Her imagined fears explained her gut feeling, but the fears didn't help her get rid of it—in fact, they made it worse. The feeling in her gut was just the aftermath of the panic. Glenda needed to instead tell herself that nothing was wrong and work on distraction and calming rather than explaining.

THE STRESS RESPONSE

Panic may drive people to the hospital thinking they're about to die even though they're not, yet few people rush to the hospital when they feel stress. However, it is being under stress that is the real killer. The stress response is an endocrinological response that gives your brain and body the energy it needs to run or fight. When that alarm goes off, your pituitary gland sends a signal through your bloodstream to your adrenal glands to release adrenaline and cortisol for mobilizing energy. This is a bit slower than the initial electric jolt of fight-or-flight that calls for a burst of adrenaline for immediate energy, and it can go on for quite some time. The adrenaline increases the intensity of your heartbeat and respiration. The cortisol tells your body to release fat and glucose for burning up if you are fighting or running. Cortisol is also the brake. When your brain receives the cortisol signal coming back and completing a feedback loop, it knows the "stress!" message has been received and stops requesting the stress response. You can see this feedback loop in Figure 2.4.

Under stress, your brain reacts, too, releasing supplies of neurotransmitters that help you respond. The neurotransmitters that regulate mood and cognition are especially affected. The stress response is dose-specific. If you have a small stress and only need a little energy, you will get a small stress response. If the stress goes on for a long time, you will get a stress response until you don't need it anymore. In other words, the duration and intensity of the stress response are determined by what kind of stress you're experiencing. And therein lies the problem. Experiencing a stress response over a period of a few minutes, as during panic, is not all that likely

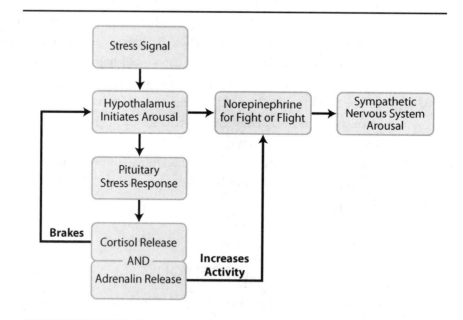

Figure 2.4 The Endocrinological Stress Response

The 10 Best-Ever Anxiety Management Techniques Workbook

to cause physical problems. But a stress response of any intensity over a period of time becomes a physical and emotional challenge.

There are several things that happen to your detriment when stress is ongoing:

- If your energy supply isn't burned off through physical exertion, such as when sitting in front of a computer 12 hours a day working to keep your business from going under, you get signals to release stores of energy that never get used. The neurochemicals prepare you for energy consumption that does not occur. This is a major reason people put fat around their middles when under stress.
- An ongoing release of adrenaline can result in adrenal fatigue, causing problems with immune functions.
- Immune activity is suppressed when you are stressed for a long period, so you may end up getting sick.
- Worse, intense and ongoing stress can lead to diseases and conditions that you are genetically susceptible to, such as diabetes type II, heart disease, and autoimmune disorders.
- If stress is severe and ongoing, the impact of all that cortisol hitting your brain can affect your ability to remember things.
- You may end up so depleted of neurotransmitters that you become depressed or anxious.

Being "stressed out" is not just a momentary unpleasantness—it is a serious health risk. And the impact on anxiety is direct. Not only do the specific conditions creating stress affect you, but the change in your health and mental functioning due to the imbalance of neurotransmitters and the other physical changes may create sensations of anxiety. Feeling anxious, you may then start to worry—a natural response to feelings of anxiety. Once your sensation of anxiety triggers worrying, you then have a feedback loop in which the anxiety and worry make each other worse, creating even more stress! (See Chapters 7 through 9 for techniques to control worry.)

THE QUANTITY AND QUALITY OF STRESS

There are two types of ongoing stress. One is related to the *quantity* of stress—when we have more to do than we can accomplish in the time we have available. For example, perhaps you have been given extra responsibilities at work, or feel pressured to take on extra responsibilities that you can't reasonably handle, both of which are common in an era of cutbacks when companies combine the work of two people into one job description—as if making it one job description will mean one person can do it all. Or perhaps you are a parent who works outside the home and must care for children when you get home after work. Single mothers are particularly vulnerable to this stress. When living with quantity stress, people tend to stop exercising, sleep too little, and stop cooking at home because the time demands seem too intense to maintain that level of self-care.

The other kind of stress has to do with its *quality*. There are times when we are under stress in an emotionally charged setting, such as when:

- We are caring for a loved one who is chronically or terminally ill
- Someone we love has died, and for months or longer we not only grieve but also have to handle legal matters or medical bills that keep resurrecting the emotions of losing that person
- We have no ability to protect a loved one who is in trouble or in danger, such as a soldier at war or someone on trial or in jail
- We are struggling to make ends meet financially and worried about how it will work out
- We suffer from oppression and poverty (people with few resources, like those who are still trying to rebuild after natural disasters, suffer from this heartrending and inescapable kind of stress)
- We suffer constant negative comparisons with others based on using social media.

People with quality stress typically feel too emotionally drained to take care of themselves well.

Whether it is quality stress or quantity stress, the lack of control you feel makes the situation feel stressful. This feeling of lack of control may stem from a very real lack of resources to correct problems, but it also can result from misperceptions. For example, you may not like your job and feel that you *must* stay at that job because if you don't, you won't have an income. You feel that you don't have a choice about it, but in truth you do—you are *choosing* the income. Seeing that you have a choice makes a big difference.

ADOLESCENTS AND STRESS

I am completely appalled at the schedules kept by many children and adolescents and equally shocked by how many parents refuse to give their children free or unscheduled time. Both teens and parents seem to believe that if they don't do every activity possible, they might miss the one and only opportunity to discover a talent or get a scholarship or entry into a good school. When I see adolescents with anxiety, I find it helpful to assess how much they are doing what they genuinely want to do versus how much they are doing because they are complying with external pressure. The following chart in Table 2.1 may help adolescents or college students see whether they have choice. Recognizing that they personally have good reasons for doing something, even if an authority also wants them to do it, can reduce the pressure. And if they are only doing it to please another person, it might be time to make a change.

DO I HAVE A CHOICE?		
What Do I Do? (list all activities)	My Reasons for Doing These Activities	My Parents', Coach's, or Teachers' Reasons

Table 2.1 Do I Have a Choice?

HOW STRESSFUL IS YOUR LIFE?

Panic isn't good for your body or your mental state, but it's not nearly as damaging as ongoing stress. So, evaluate your stress here and then pay careful attention to the lifestyle changes discussed in Chapters 3 through 6.

How Stressful Is Your Life?

Give yourself the number of points indicated for items that apply to you.

Changes at work:
_____ Change in type of work or major change in job expectations (1)
_____ Change in coworkers (2)
_____ Change in boss or supervisor (3)
_____ Change in career (4)
Score _____

Changes in living:
_____ Moved to a new home within same city (1)
_____ Moved to a different city within same country (2)
_____ Moved to another country (3)
Score _____

Changes in finances:
_____ Took a cut in pay (1)
_____ Living in a more expensive area (2)
_____ Sending children to a more expensive school (3)
_____ Have incurred credit card debt that cannot be quickly paid off (4)
_____ Took a new mortgage (5)
Score _____

Changes in personal life:
_____ Began a new important relationship (1)
_____ Believe your personal life must be kept private for your well-being at work (2)
_____ Got married (3)
_____ Had a child (4)
_____ Living separately from your spouse who is in another location (5)
_____ Living with a person who creates serious problems for your well-being (e.g., is persistently verbally berating; is often emotionally distraught and shows it in tearful, angry, or frightening outbursts; or is addicted to substances and you must interact with that person while he or she is under the influence and put up with the person's stealing, accidents, or physical consequences of the addiction) (6)
Score _____

Changes in health:
_____ Had a short-term illness that caused you to miss a few days of work (2)

_____ Are undergoing tests to determine cause of symptoms, without positive tests (4)

_____ Had a serious illness that caused you to miss many days of work (6)

_____ Have a chronic illness that affects your energy and overall feeling of wellness (8)

_____ Have a newly diagnosed, serious chronic illness that is not terminal (10)

Score _____

Losses:

(*Note: It is difficult to numerically rate the emotional upset caused by losses. For example, a person who has relied on a service dog may grieve the loss of that animal as a beloved family member, whereas someone without a strong feeling toward a family pet may bounce back quickly. Likewise, the loss of an extended family member could be experienced as grievous or only mild. Furthermore, emotional and financial support resources—or lack thereof— may have an effect. If you have experienced any of the following losses, rate it on a scale of 1 to 13, with 1 being very mild loss and 13 being grievous loss.*)

_____ Loss of a beloved pet

_____ Diminishing health of a parent for whom you provide some care

_____ Living with a parent or child with serious, chronic health problems

_____ Death of a mother, father, or sibling

_____ Death of a child

_____ Death of an extended family member

_____ Death of a friend or coworker

_____ Death of a spouse

_____ Divorce

_____ Loss of home due to foreclosure

_____ Loss of job

Score _____

Total of all scores _____

1–9 points = Stress in your life is happening. Maintain good self-care, as always.

10–12 points = Yellow caution zone. Stress is taking a toll and you need to pay special attention to replenishing your energy so you don't become exhausted.

13 points or more = Red zone. Reach out for help and support. This is when people tend to get sick or have accidents. Be especially careful about sleep and nutrition, take your vitamins, and seek and accept help of all types wherever it is available.

Every stressful period can result in growth or loss, depending on how you care for yourself during this time. But if too many stresses pile up and you don't get assistance or take care of yourself, you may suffer losses in relationships and in your physical and mental well-being. If you are the type of person who tends to take on way too much responsibility and downplays the effect stress is having in your life, pay particular attention to the techniques in Chapter 11.

HAS IT ALREADY GONE ON TOO LONG?

Are you showing signs of destructive stress? Take the following test to see if you have indications that stress is negatively affecting you.

A FINAL WORD

Once you have a sense of the stress you're experiencing, you may find that you are stymied about how to change the level of stress. I have found that when people have serious life stress, they lose perspective and may need an outside person to help them see ways to decrease their level of stress or get some help. The good news is that proper self-care will help alleviate the negative impact of stress.

Pay careful attention to your nutrition, exercise, and sleep. See my book *The 10 Best-Ever Anxiety Management Techniques* for a longer discussion of those needs, and check out the Resources section at the end of this book.

Is Stress Negatively Affecting You?

Check off the physical signs of stress that you are experiencing regularly:

☐ Headaches
☐ Muscle pain, especially back pain
☐ Indigestion
☐ Diarrhea
☐ Appetite changes
☐ Jaw tightening, tooth grinding, TMJ
☐ Weakness and fatigue
☐ Insomnia

Check off the emotional signs of stress that are you experiencing regularly:

☐ You become irritable or grouchy over little things
☐ You are easily angered
☐ You feel anxiety that you can't resolve
☐ You feel as if everything that might have been fun is now a burden to do
☐ You experience frequent loss of concentration
☐ You make more mistakes at work than usual
☐ You are accident prone
☐ You feel frozen about where to start each day or each activity

Check off the signs of poor self-care that are you experiencing regularly:

☐ You have stopped exercise regimens
☐ You are eating more food or more junk food
☐ You are experiencing weight gain, especially around your middle
☐ You are drinking more alcohol to relax
☐ You are drinking more caffeine to get going in the morning
☐ You are not dressing with as much care
☐ You are paying less attention to your personal appearance, such as tidy clothing or makeup
☐ You have decreased your leisure time and pleasant contact with friends or family

Total items checked: _____

0–3 = You are sailing along without serious effects of stress and should teach others how you do it!

4–5 = Stress is starting to interfere with your health or well-being. Take some self-care steps.

6–8 = Reevaluate now! Stress is affecting your well-being.

8 or more = Talk to someone immediately about how to diminish your stress today.

PART II

Managing Your Anxious Body

THREE

Technique #1
Change Your Intake

Changing your intake—from the kinds of food you eat to how often you check your phone—is a key feature in managing the physiology of anxiety. Whether you have panic attacks, acute anxiety, or that sick feeling of having made a social gaffe, you feel anxiety in your body. These physical feelings can be triggered by something as simple as drinking a cup of coffee—but your brain doesn't always recognize this. It may instead jump to the conclusion that you are having these physical sensations because there is something very real that you need to be worried about, and it will begin making up reasons to explain why you feel so physically anxious. This chapter will help your brain notice the connection between your intake and feelings of anxiety or panic.

ASSESS YOUR INTAKE OF C.A.T.S.

C.A.T.S. stands for caffeine, alcohol, tobacco, and sugar and sweeteners. If you have the physical sensations of anxiety, the first step of assessment (after you consult a physician) is to assess your level of C.A.T.S. intake.

Track Anxiety Related to Caffeine and Sugar and Sweeteners

The first appraisal is easy: Write down what you eat and drink, and then set a timer for 45 minutes and check how you feel. Are caffeine, sugar, or other specific foods triggering anxiety sensations? Josiah was a college senior who suffered from panic. He thought it was the outcome of stress, and heaven knows, he had a lot of it—internships, taking lots of credits, and working for money besides all this. But as we looked at the origin of his panic, he could see that it started when he was chronically short on sleep and began using energy drinks and copious amounts of espresso to keep going. By the time he hit spring break, he was suffering from intense panic attacks and even had been evaluated for heart problems despite his age. He was stunned when abstinence from caffeine (and practicing anxiety management) helped him resume his school life without panic attacks.

A much younger client, Matt, began to suffer from anxiety in his sophomore year of high school. He was a self-described "sugar-holic," and he described anxiety coming over him like a descending fog. But, by tracking, we found that his anxiety could be predicted. When he ate doughnuts for breakfast or skipped lunch in favor of a candy bar, he would feel that sense of dread within 45 minutes.

Because sensitivity varies greatly from person to person, only you can tell whether certain foods and drinks are causing your anxiety symptoms. The best way to do this is by tracking how you feel after eating or drinking. You may also note that some foods produce feelings other than anxiety: you may feel sleepy, jittery, energized, mellow, alert, and so on. That might help you assess the impact of your food intake in general.

Anxiety/Panic Before and After Food and Drink Consumption

Rate your anxiety/panic from 1 to 10, with 1 being low and 10 intense.

Level of Anxiety/Panic Before I Eat	What I Ate/Drank	Level of Anxiety/Panic 45 Minutes After I Eat
3 – a little worried feeling	large coffee with cream	7 – feeling like something's wrong
4 – not back to morning level	hot dog and fries	3 – busy at work so am distracted from worry
3 – still distracted from thoughts	large cola	8 – feels like dread now, but the boss asked me to stay late
5 – but I worked late and rushed home	fish filet, green beans, and brown rice; water/decaf tea	3 – feel calmer but still worried about how much work I have

Figure 3.1 Anxiety/Panic Before and After Food and Drink Consumption

The 10 Best-Ever Anxiety Management Techniques Workbook

Anxiety/Panic Before and After Food and Drink Consumption

Rate your anxiety/panic from 1 to 10, with 1 being low and 10 intense.

Level of Anxiety/Panic Before I Eat	What I Ate/Drank	Level of Anxiety/Panic 45 Minutes After I Eat

Notes: _____

_____

_____

_____

Use the following chart to track the foods and drinks you consume, and then rate your anxiety (or panic) levels on a scale of 1 to 10, with 1 being low and 10 being intense. A sample chart is provided first (Figure 3.1), with a blank one for you to fill out after that. You can also use an index card or your mobile device to keep track. There are many food-tacking apps, but their focus is on calories or food type consumed without many options for noting how you feel, but go ahead and use one if you find one that works. For most of us, technology makes tracking easier. Just make sure you track your intake over several days so you can identify any consistent effects on your anxiety or panic.

Track Anxiety Related to Alcohol

Many people use alcohol to calm down, and that may work. But alcohol can cause problems with anxiety, panic, and restless sleep. Even a relatively small amount of alcohol may disrupt your sleep pattern, and this lack of sleep can contribute to anxiety. Binge drinking or drinking to the point of drunkenness, as many young adults do, can lead to problems not only with anxiety but also with alcohol dependence. But there is so much connection here that I believe it is the cause of what young people note in #Sundaysadness—the awareness that Sunday afternoon prompts worry and depression about returning to classes or work. It may be the outcome of the Saturday socializing instead!

Is alcohol contributing to your panic or anxiety? Keep a "day after" diary to find out. Every time you consume alcohol, note how much you are drinking and the time of day. In the morning, rate your quality of sleep on a scale from 1 (excellent) to 10 (poor). At the end of the day, rate the intensity of anxiety (or occurrence of panic attacks) you experienced throughout the day, again using a scale of 1 (low intensity) to 10 (high intensity). Do this for several occasions of using alcohol to see if there is consistent pattern. Is your anxiety worse the day after drinking? Then decide if you want to stop using alcohol in that way.

Break Into Your Cigarette Break

Everyone knows it's a good idea to stop smoking, and anxious smokers know that smoking is hard to give up. When I talk to people with anxiety about why they smoke, especially after they quit and are a bit more honest with themselves, they consistently talk about the cigarette allowing them to get away from anxiety-provoking situations or just take a break that they wouldn't otherwise allow themselves. If they can't justify sitting down for five minutes, they can justify it with a cigarette. Now that almost every building is nonsmoking, the break is really a break by the time you leave and find a spot where the smoke is accepted.

Techniques to quit smoking are beyond the scope of this book, but breaking into your cigarette break can help get you on the right path. It's basically about developing ways to get a break that don't require cigarettes and learning to differentiate nicotine craving from anxiety. Once you can get a break without a smoke, you will be better set up to quit smoking entirely when you decide to take that step.

First, you will need some ideas about how to get a little break, whether at home or work, that are specifically good for you and your setting. List five things you can do for two to five minutes that feel relaxing. For example:

Alcohol Intake "Day After" Diary

In the left-hand column, note the number of drinks you had and the time of day you consumed them. In the middle column, rate the quality of sleep you experienced that night, with 1 being excellent and 10 being poor. In the right-hand column, rate your anxiety/panic from1 to 10, with 1 being low and 10 intense.

	Sleep Quality	Level of Anxiety/Panic
Day 1 *Number of drinks:* _____ *Time of day:* _____		
Day 2 *Number of drinks:* _____ *Time of day:* _____		
Day 3 *Number of drinks:* _____ *Time of day:* _____		
Day 4 *Number of drinks:* _____ *Time of day:* _____		
Day 5 *Number of drinks:* _____ *Time of day:* _____		
Day 6 *Number of drinks:* _____ *Time of day:* _____		
Day 7 *Number of drinks:* _____ *Time of day:* _____		

- Diaphragmatic breathing
- Walking up and down the stairs a few times
- Texting (or even better speaking with) your spouse or partner on the phone
- Looking at pictures of your last vacation
- Stretching

You will use these as a way to get a little break before you smoke. See Figure 3.2.

Break Into Your Cigarette Break

Whenever you feel like you need a cigarette, follow the steps below.

1. Rate your anxiety level from 1 to 10, with 10 being highest: _____
2. Choose an item from your list of relaxing activities and do it.
3. Now, again rate your anxiety level from 1 to 10: _____
4. Now ask yourself, "Do I still want nicotine?" If the answer is yes, then take the cigarette for the nicotine, not for the relaxation break.

Figure 3.2 Break Into Your Cigarette Break

TECHNOLOGICAL COMMUNICATION STRESS

Technology improves our lives in many ways, but it also contributes to stress. Not all of us learn new technologies intuitively, so when software changes at work or at home, it may leave you feeling frustrated or confounded, and the consequences of not learning new programs can be severe. Those who need training face the stress of getting it in a timely way. In the rapidly developing world of mobile technologies and apps and social media, the numbers of people who competently handle technology is increasing. If we are lucky, those of us who are older and find it harder can turn to young family members to help out!

Now the stress of technology seems to have shifted from using it at all to using it too much. And the cause is primarily our own ability to limit our involvement. One issue is the sheer volume of data. Our brains have not yet evolved to keep up with what could be a never-ending stream of access to information. Sorting through this is stressful. When do you stop searching online for information? When is posting on or reading social media enough to prove your interest in your friends? When do you stop doing work from mobile devices after you leave work for the day? When will your colleagues stop clogging your work in-box by hitting "reply all" to prove they are on top of things at work??? If you don't put your own limits on it, communication through all the means at your disposal can cut into your time to relax, your ability to sleep, and your sense of connection to other people.

Ferris Jabr, in a 2013 article for *Scientific American Mind*, summarized research about the significance of mental rest:

> Downtime replenishes the brain's stores of attention and motivation, encourages productivity and creativity, and is essential to both achieve

our highest levels of performance and simply form stable memories in everyday life. A wandering mind unsticks us in time so that we can learn from the past and plan for the future. Moments of respite may even be necessary to keep one's moral compass in working order and maintain a sense of self.

That is a beautiful description of why you must evaluate your capacity to take a break.

This is the chapter on changing your intake. So, consider your intake of communication. If you are under any stress at all, consider whether some of these typical stressors affect you:

Email. Before the advent of email, people actually stopped working when they left work. Today, almost everyone who uses email is still taking work-related messages at all times of the day. This interferes with quality sleep and getting other work done. One young man who felt a lot of anxiety in general described his evening as "not having enough time to relax." Evaluating his pattern, he realized that he was sitting with his family with the TV on, but he was returning email from work while he did so. He never felt as if that family TV time was relaxing. He still believed he had to do some work, so he decided to take 30 to 60 minutes of quiet time to respond to messages and then joined his family for a couple of hours. He quickly noticed that the downtime with his family was far more relaxing without the work in front of him.

Answering calls and texts. The compulsion to answer incoming calls during face-to-face meetings or family activity time (like meals, shopping, or riding together in the car) is very strong. This is so endemic at every age in our society that it is common to see families or friend groups out socially yet giving all their attention to their devices. To address this, one foursome of friends has decided to put their mobile phones on the table when they eat out, and the first one to pick theirs up has to pay the tab. They have made a line in the sand—time together is time together, and you will pay if you interrupt it! When one of them starts getting calls on their wristwatch, that will pose new challenges—will "peeking at it" constitute a violation that makes them pay the fine?

The ubiquitous notification signal. Whether the signal is chiming, dinging, buzzing, or beeping, your brain registers it as a demand. You get a little squirt of dopamine—the feel-good neurochemical—when you know someone wants your attention. But your brain keeps you on edge until you check it. Find times to turn off notifications—like overnight or while you are spending time at a meal.

The stress of texting instead of talking. Even when we're in a real conversation with full access to a person's tone of voice, face, and posture, we have misunderstandings. If our filters don't work perfectly with all that information, just consider what is likely to go wrong when you have only words. You imbue them with whatever tone of voice you imagine, regardless of how the writer intended the message.

But we all know the temptation to text. It's fast; there's no need to listen to a voicemail; it's so quiet that you can do it in the quiet car of the commuter train; parents don't hear the voices of their teens having conversations in the middle of the night when they should be sleeping. Although the emotional pain of fighting by text or breaking up by text is as real as in a verbal encounter and you lose the benefit of getting the whole story of face and tone that might allow for understanding, you can avoid personal responsibility for hurting the receiver. When adolescents answered Sherry Turkle's query (see her book *Alone Together*) about what they liked about texting their parents instead of talking to them, one of the main reasons was a sense of control (i.e., less stress)—texting limited parental verbiage and allowed the adolescents to choose when to reply. In a couple of paragraphs, I am going to discuss "demand delays," and this is certainly one example!

The sheer volume of information you are expected to respond to. You may experience stress from daily facing the challenge of finding important facts buried in the amount of irrelevant data available to you, or you may have information overload due to the amount of *seemingly* important information that you already know that you will never remember. The volume takes a toll on your ability to concentrate and remember and adds the stress of identifying what is worth trying to remember.

The impact of social media. This deserves a book, and I don't have to write it here because Sherry Turkle has already written not one but three on the topic. Her most recent one came out in 2016 and is called *Reclaiming Conversation*. Her work is excellent and worth a read. But you can begin to think about what kind of stress the ever-changing technology of social media adds to your life. It can't be ignored as its own source of both positive connections and stress. Examine and evaluate the impact of your use of these media, which currently include Facebook and much faster apps like Snapchat, WhatsApp, Instagram, and Twitter.

- Do you feel jealous or judged when you are using these options to communicate?
- Do you find yourself losing time every day when you go to a site and suddenly realize you have spent far more time than intended?
- Do you find yourself becoming angry at the kinds of posts others put up?

- Do you get tired of how perfect everyone else's life seems?
- Do you feel agitated if you can't get on a site to see what's up?

Create Demand Delays

Creating "demand delays" is about (1) assessing your level of technological communication stress by seeing how anxious it makes you to delay your responses to these demands for attention and (2) ultimately being in control of demands to spend your day communicating this way.

First, make a deliberate choice to limit your availability to answer texts, emails, and messages via Facebook, LinkedIn, and all the many other means, including dating sites, and see how your anxiety level changes. Following are a few ideas based in time management research; choose the one that fits best with your work and personal life.

- Wait to check your email for at least an hour into your workday. Try getting some work done first.
- Check your voicemail, take messages, and return calls at specific times in your day when it suits your schedule best.
- Turn off everything at home that rings or dings, including cell phones, while you eat your meal. Make mealtimes a "no-call zone."
- Turn off your mobile device during face-to-face meetings or put notification signals on silent, including eliminating the vibrate function.
- Leave your cell phone in the car when you go into a restaurant, or put it on silent, not vibrate, so that your attention is completely on your meal and your companions. (Do the same thing in theaters, meetings, churches, lectures, and so on.) Consider borrowing the plan of the four friends who pay a price if they break the rule!
- If you carry a specific mobile device connected to work, take it off when you're not on call.
- If you are required to take a computer home or to work from home, make a specific agreement with your supervisor about exactly which hours you are expected to work. Don't respond to messages from work except during those hours.
- If you're going to work from home, don't work while also trying to watch a program or talk to those with whom you live. You will spend less time getting the work done and will get more benefit from the relaxation.

Once you've selected one of these delays, try it for at least a week. Each day, rate your anxiety level, both during the delay time and after it, on a scale of 1 to 10. At the end of the week, look at the chart to see how your anxiety level changed over the course of the week. You will probably find that as you got more used to doing the delay, your anxiety went down. Figure 3.3 shows a sample chart; use the blank one after that to track your own response to demand delays.

As your anxiety levels go down with demand delays, you will become more able to take the breaks you need during the day. When it comes to energy output, people are energetically tuned to sprint and then relax. That is why marathon training is for the few and the hardy! You will function with less anxiety if you take time to recover from the intake of tension generated by too much time with your work technology. Especially for those of you who work at desks with computers, try taking two minutes per hour to replenish the energy expended throughout the day by taking a break to stand and stretch or move around so you can transform a marathon into a series of sprints.

Of course, you may also be using technology compulsively in an effort to take a break from work—much like smokers use cigarette breaks to "relax." Responding to every ding and ring from your mobile or email inbox may be your way of trying to gain relief from the stress of getting a work or school project done. If this is the case, follow the suggestions for taking a break in the section titled "Break Into Your Cigarette

Demand Delay: *Wait 1 hour to do email at work*

Each day, rate your anxiety level, both during the delay time and after it, on a scale of 1 to 10, with 1 being low and 10 being high.

	Anxiety Level During Demand Delay	Anxiety Level After Demand Delay
Day 1	8	2
Day 2	7	3
Day 3	5	2
Day 4	4	1
Day 5	2	1

Figure 3.3 Demand Delay

The 10 Best-Ever Anxiety Management Techniques Workbook

Demand Delay: _____

Each day, rate your anxiety level, both during the delay time and after it, on a scale of 1 to 10, with 1 being low and 10 being high.

	Anxiety Level During Demand Delay	Anxiety Level After Demand Delay
Day 1		
Day 2		
Day 3		
Day 4		
Day 5		

Notes: _____

_____

_____

_____

Break." Spending a few minutes stretching, looking at pictures, or doing diaphragmatic breathing can be more relaxing than compulsively checking your messages.

The downloadable audio track called "Balancing Breath" and "Lengthening the Exhale" offers two types of breathing to help you take a short break no matter where you are:

The Quantity of Technological Communication Stress

As I explained above, the demands of technology may be too much for you to keep up with. When you can't entirely avoid these technology demands, you must pick a logical way to slow them down, control them, or interrupt them. Use your demand delays chart to help you decide what arena you want to address first. There are many possibilities, but the categories shown in Figure 3.4 might help you focus on the next step to alleviating techno stress.

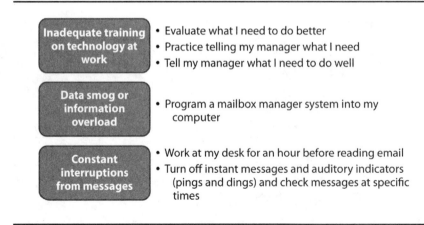

Figure 3.4 Ideas to Manage Quantity Techno Stress

Quality of Technological Communication Stress

Constantly dividing your awareness between what you are doing in the present moment and incoming messages brings its own kind of stress. If you want to reduce technological communication stress, start by becoming aware of how it affects the quality of your life and your relationships. For example, you may not have noticed that your time with your children or your spouse is compromised by constant messaging with people who aren't present. You can lose out on fully experiencing the moment—such as at a child's ballet recital—when you divide your attention by answering work emails and texts. Memory requires focus and concentration. When information is meaningful, it is easier to hold on to it. Continuous partial attention disrupts your ability to appreciate meaning. If you want to improve your memory and concentration for personal connections, you would do well to reduce the continuous partial-attention energy drain of watching your phone. Some familiar problems occur:

- For students whose work is learning. If you are a stressed-out student, you may find that your anxiety skyrockets when you are separated from you peers by turning off your mobile, but once you get used to it, you will find that your studies are faster and easier and have better results. You will remember more, more easily, if you focus on one task at a time.
- For people who work from home. It can be challenging to establish boundaries between personal work and office work. The pressure of undone work in either arena creates the "never-finished" phenomenon.

Work from home means always working	• Create a totally separate work place • Before leaving the home office, turn off the computer monitor, then take three deep breaths
Divided attention makes for ineffeciency	• Create uninterrupted stretches of time in which to focus on one task • Turn off notification signals while working
Distraction in meetings or in social settings	• Turn off cell phones in social or work meetings

Figure 3.5 Ideas to Manage Quality Techno Stress

When technology tethers you to it and you feel the stress of never getting away from it, you must evaluate what work you can turn off and for how long. It will be a relief to stay focused on the people around you at home. But it also means leaving home problems behind for work time. It's helpful to make clear delineations between work time and home time. One way to do this is to create a specific ritual—even just a short one—to use when you go from work time to home time or vice versa. You might take a series of deep breaths, change your shoes, or use the clear-the-mind technique (The audio track "Contain Your Worry") when you switch between your home and your home office.

• For people who come home with work on their mind. The ideas listed above are helpful here as well. I would suggest using the clear-the-mind technique as you leave home or leave work so that your commute can be a genuine transition, during which you can listen to music or the news or read or do some other nonwork, nonhome task. If you aren't driving, this transition can be time to connect with others. Here is one blessing of technology! Some other ideas for managing quality technological communication stress are shown in Figure 3.5.

Physical, Mental, and Interpersonal Recovery Drills

Taking breaks to alleviate stress during work, no matter where you are working, relieves both your body and your brain. Try the ideas in Figure 3.6 for two-minute relaxation breaks for physical, mental, and interpersonal recovery. Once you decide which of these ideas works best with your work setting and personal preferences, set up a routine in which you take the two-minute break every 90 minutes. Set a reminder on your computer or phone so you don't forget.

All of these drills can be adapted for children coming home from school, too. Most school counselors will have ideas about how to give a child some breaks at school during the day, so be sure to consult with the counselor if you think your child could use break time during the school day.

Physical Recovery Drills

Get relief from technology by calming your body.

Breath awareness or diaphragmatic breathing
Hydration (most of us do not drink enough water compared to other beverages)
Exercise ("desk yoga" or taking a 2-minute walk)
Progressive muscle relaxation
Aromas
Healthy snacks, eaten mindfully
Computer-generated biofeedback mechanism (see Appendix for information on devices like Heartmath, Stress Eraser, and Wild Divine)

Mental Recovery Drills

Getting away in your mind can be a relief from techno intensity.

Relaxation, meditation, or guided imagery (use earphones to listen if you don't have an office where you can shut the door)
Music (a listening experience that affects mood and tension levels)
Photos (use digital picture frames or screensavers for visual self-soothing; while looking at the photos, contemplate associated memories of people and places)

Interpersonal Recovery Drills

Connecting with others is comforting!

Call a significant other to say hello
Meet a coworker at the water fountain/kitchen for a quick cup of tea
Acknowledge someone who has done a good job or worked hard

Figure 3.6 Physical, Mental, and Interpersonal Recovery Drills

Sensitive Children and Stress

Children who have sensitive temperaments and are responsive to noise or confusion, as many children with social anxiety are, need to have ways to calm down or get breaks.

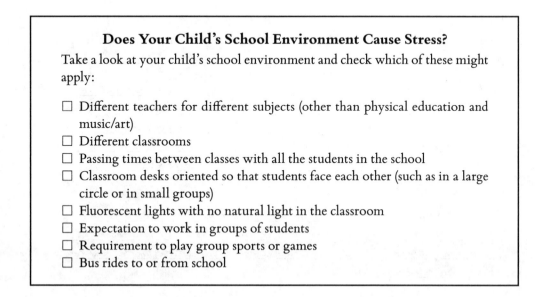

Does Your Child's School Environment Cause Stress?

Take a look at your child's school environment and check which of these might apply:

☐ Different teachers for different subjects (other than physical education and music/art)
☐ Different classrooms
☐ Passing times between classes with all the students in the school
☐ Classroom desks oriented so that students face each other (such as in a large circle or in small groups)
☐ Fluorescent lights with no natural light in the classroom
☐ Expectation to work in groups of students
☐ Requirement to play group sports or games
☐ Bus rides to or from school

All of these can place demands on sensitive children, tiring them or prompting resistance when there are too many points of stress. Confusion and environmental noise or stimulation can be exhausting. See if there are ways to create quiet zones for your child, like a reading space away from the hubbub. If that's not possible, be sure that there is some time after school for the child to calm down. Use the ideas from the recovery drills in the previous section to create recovery breaks for the child.

THE S.I.M.P.L.E. PLAN FOR INTERVENING ON INTAKE

This part is simple, but not easy. Start with whichever arena of intake seemed most relevant, whether it be food, alcohol, cigarettes, or technology, and set up a S.I.M.P.L.E. plan to eliminate or replace one of them. It's important to start with just one, because even if you think you should intervene in every arena of intake, doing just one at a time allows you to observe the impact of that specific change

S.I.M.P.L.E. Plan to Change Intake
(minimizing caffeine intake)

S: What is the situation or symptom? *I have a lot of jitteriness and anxious feelings that seem to be worse when I drink caffeine.*

I: What is the impact on my life? *It makes it hard for me to feel good, but I drink a lot of coffee to stay alert and I drink diet cola when I am not drinking coffee. I probably drink four cans of cola per day.*

M: What *method* am I trying? *I am going to give up caffeine slowly. I am going to eliminate any caffeine after 3pm. I am going to drink only half-caf coffee and I am going to limit myself to two colas per day. I will do this for a week, then I will go to one cola/day. After 2 weeks, I will drink half-caf coffee only in the morning and none for the rest of the day.*

P: Practice plan. *I am going to have a hard time with the no caffeine after 3 at work. I will try no caffeine in the afternoon on the weekend first and see if there is another beverage I could substitute, like herbal tea or a no-caffeine cold drink.*

L: Lifework. *I will write my goals down and put them someplace where I see them frequently, like on a Post-It stuck to my bathroom mirror or in the Outlook program on my computer.*

E: Evaluate. *I will track my anxiety level at noon and at dinnertime every day for 3 weeks to see if there is an observable impact on my anxiety. I will set my timer in my phone to remind me to check in with myself.*

Figure 3.7 S.I.M.P.L.E. Plan to Change Intake (minimizing caffeine intake)

and better understand which kind of intake is prompting your anxiety or panic. Changing only one thing at a time will also make you feel less stressed out about change!

It's also important to take care in filling out the "evaluation" part of the chart. Evaluating the results of your changes will strengthen your resolve to continue positive changes in your intake.

S.I.M.P.L.E. Plan to Change Intake
(separating craving a cigarette from craving a break)

S: What is the *symptom* or *situation*? *I step outside to smoke when I feel anxiety at work.*

I: What is the *impact* on my life? *It is inconvenient, especially in bad weather, but it also gives me a really good reason to leave work and be away for a few minutes.*

M: What *method* am I trying? *I am going to try stretching in the break room or the bathroom for 2 minutes before I decide to have a cigarette. I am going to rate my anxiety level before I walk away from my workstation and after I stretch.*

P: Practice plan. *I can try this out for a week and see if anyone notices what I am doing.*

L: Lifework. *I will develop several different methods so that I can have some choices for how to take a break depending on where I am and what the weather is like.*

E: Evaluate. *I will note whether I want a cigarette as badly after I stretch. I will evaluate whether I want to decrease cigarette consumption and also whether I smoke less this way.*

Figure 3.8 S.I.M.P.L.E. Plan to Change Intake
(separating craving a cigarette from craving a break)

Your homework for changing your intake can be set up with a S.I.M.P.L.E. plan, which stands for the process of planning. Identify the *situation*, note the *impact* it has on your life, clarify the *method* you are going to use, *practice* your plan, set goals for *lifework*, and *evaluate* how it works or should be modified. Figures 3.7 and 3.8 offer a couple of sample S.I.M.P.L.E. charts and are followed by a blank chart for you to fill out.

S.I.M.P.L.E. Plan to Change Intake

S: What is the *symptom* or *situation*? _____

_____

_____

I: What is the impact on my life? _____

_____

_____

M: What *method* am I trying? _____

_____

_____

P: *Practice* plan. _____

_____

_____

L: *Lifework.*_____

_____

_____

E: *Evaluate.* _____

_____

_____

A FINAL WORD

Understanding what aspects of intake are increasing your anxiety level will suggest easy pathways to reducing the physiological symptoms of anxiety. Whether you suffer from panic, generalized anxiety, or even social anxiety, relieving sources of agitation and stress may decrease your level of anxiety and prepare you to benefit more from the other techniques in this workbook.

FOUR

Technique #2
Breathe

This technique is the most important one you will ever use to control the physical side of anxiety. It can completely eliminate panic, soothe general anxiety, and keep you calmer when facing social situations so that you can do your best in them.

I find that if people understand why this technique works, they are more willing to try it and more willing to practice. Right now, go ahead and do one simple thing: take a deep, slow breath, and let it go. Were you aware of your breathing before reading that suggestion? Probably not. Why? It would be impossible to function if you were aware of all of your body's automatic functions. We breathe all day without a conscious thought about it. Your body and brain work together to keep you breathing just the right amount, and it never interferes with other things you should be thinking or doing. However, the very moment you decide to breathe, your conscious thought takes over the automatic function of breathing, and you are in control.

Panic begins with *unconscious activity* in your brain that initiates the sudden rise of heart rate, an increase in respiration, and other physical changes that prepare you for fight-or-flight. The moment you are aware that panic could start or is under way, you can make your breathing conscious and take control of your panic by controlling your breath. You might remember from Chapter 2 that your nervous system can't be revved up and slowed down at the same time. When you simply start to breathe slowly, the brain-body functions that slow you down take over. Your whole body starts to slow down.

The sensation of generalized anxiety is also caused by unconscious activity. You may feel a sense of dread or impending trouble. You may have tension building even when you're not aware of it until you feel tied in knots. This kind of physical experience of anxiety, which is often accompanied by worrying, causes you to have a physical reaction. Even though it doesn't cause the same dramatic spike in heart rate and respiration as panic, those fight-or-flight physical responses still kick in, and conscious breathing can be used to calm them.

ASSESS YOUR BREATH

The next time you are under pressure—perhaps during a meeting in which you have to speak or during a disagreement with someone—set aside a part of your attention to observe how your breathing changes when you are tense. It may surprise you to find that you have not been filling your lungs or that you have been holding your breath. Fill out the following chart, putting a check next to all the items that describe your breathing in these stressful situations and adding any other observations you may have.

Assess Your Breath

Type of Breath	✓	Type of Breath	✓
Short or impeded intake *Notes:*		Even, but fast *Notes:*	
Gasping *Notes:*		Relaxed *Notes:*	
Long in, short out *Notes:*		Holding breath *Notes:*	
Shallow *Notes:*		Panting *Notes:*	
Gulping *Notes:*		Hyperventilating *Notes:*	

The 10 Best-Ever Anxiety Management Techniques Workbook

LEARN DIAPHRAGMATIC BREATHING

Taking just one deep breath and letting it go will help relieve some stress, but breathing to control panic works better if you do the method called "diaphragmatic breathing" (Figure 4.1). This is a different type of breath than the short, shallow, panting respirations common to panic. It is sometimes referred to as "belly breathing." When you breathe in this way, you exert control over the pace at which you inhale and exhale.

Diaphragmatic Breathing

Getting Started

1. Lie down flat on your back or stand in a relaxed manner, feet slightly apart, knees loose. This is so you can sense the movement in your abdomen, which should move out when you inhale and pull in when you exhale.
2. Rest your hand on your abdomen. This will help you to notice if you are breathing deeply enough and whether your chest is tight.
3. Next, exhale the air in your lungs so you are completely empty to start the practice.
4. Now, breathe in through your nose. Inhaling must be done evenly, as if you can fill your lungs from bottom to top in equal, even amounts. One way to imagine this is to think about how a balloon fills with water when you attach it to a faucet. The bottom fills and widens first and then the water expands the upper portion. This image of heaviness as you fill suggests how to imagine your breath. Form an image of your breath filling a balloon in your abdomen, becoming heavy and warm as you inhale.

Finding the Right Pace for You

5. As you inhale, count in your mind as you breathe in. The pace of counting does not matter, as long as you do it at the same pace every time. You might try a pace of one second per count. Count until you feel exactly full (e.g., a slow 1, 2, 3, 4) to help you get a measured, even breath. Chances are you will take between 3 to 6 counts to fill your lungs with smooth inhalations.
6. Then, exhale evenly, taking longer than you did to inhale, at a slow pace until your lungs feel empty. The pace of exhaling should be slow and steady. Imagine you are blowing at the flame of a candle enough to move it but not blow it out. Your body needs time to exchange the oxygen and carbon dioxide or you can get dizzy—a symptom you are trying to eliminate, not encourage!
7. If you are getting dizzy, exhale for two counts longer or pause for two counts at the end of the exhalation of your breath before you start to inhale again.
8. When you find the right pace, write it down. You will use this number to tally practice sessions a bit later. You may find that the pace you like when you are relaxed is different from the pace you like when you are anxious, so make notes about those differences. You may use one pace for breathing to relax and one pace for controlling panic or anxiety.

Figure 4.1 Diaphragmatic Breathing

Even though this way of breathing is about conscious control over an otherwise automatic process, it's not just using your conscious effort. Rather, when you breathe with the slow inhale through the nose and the longer exhale through the mouth, you stimulate the automatic action of the *parasympathetic nervous system*. This part of your nervous system acts without conscious intention to slow your heart rate and respiration and lower your blood pressure and allows your digestive process to get back to normal. All of that is initiated by diaphragmatic breathing and reverses the automatic arousal of panic and acute anxiety. Your exhale is what makes the most difference to this breath working well. That is why you exhale longer than you inhale. The ideal ratio is to exhale twice as long as you inhale, but that can be hard to do. You may try a pause between the outbreath and the inbreath to lengthen that interval more comfortably.

Follow the guidelines in Figure 4.1, and practice breathing the first time by lying down or standing—after that, you can do this type of breathing anywhere without anyone noticing. Be aware that the goal is not to change the way you breathe as you go about your daily activities but rather to consciously change the way you breathe when you begin to feel panic or anxiety coming on.

Make a Record of Your Breathing Pace

Again, the pace you find right for diaphragmatic breathing while relaxed and practicing may be different from the one that works best during stressful situations. Making a record of these differences can be helpful. Figure 4.2 shows a sample record, followed by one for you to fill out.

The main point is taking control of your breath and slowing it. When you do that, you initiate calming throughout your whole nervous system.

	My Pace for Breathing When I Am Practicing	My Pace for Breathing When I Am Anxious
Inhale	1, 2, 3, 4, 5	1, 2, 3
Exhale	1, 2, 3, 4, 5, 6, 7	1, 2, 3
Pause	1, 2	1

Figure 4.2 Diaphragmatic Breathing Pace

The 10 Best-Ever Anxiety Management Techniques Workbook

	My Pace for Breathing When I Am Practicing	My Pace for Breathing When I Am Anxious
Inhale		
Exhale		
Pause		

Create "Breathing Minutes"

If you want diaphragmatic breathing to work, you will have to master it and then remember to do it! The best way to guarantee that is to practice. You can listen to the audio track, "Diaphragmatic Breathing," to help you learn and practice breathing. The most effective practice I know involves creating "breathing minutes." For 1 minute at a time, 10 to 15 times a day, practice diaphragmatic breathing. You don't need to be standing or lying down—a good time to practice is whenever you are waiting for something. For example, practice breathing when you are:

- Stopped at a traffic light
- On hold on the phone
- Waiting in line at a store
- Waiting for the next play while watching a sporting event on TV
- Waiting for the microwave to heat some food
- Waiting for a friend at work or school
- Waiting in the car to pick up someone
- Waiting for the computer to boot
- Waiting for the teacher to hand out the test papers
- Waiting for a text message
- Waiting for a meeting to start

Some people prefer to set a timer on their watch, phone, or computer, and when it dings they start breathing for a minute. The more often you practice, the more likely you are to use this technique.

Finally, keeping a tally of the number of breathing minutes you practice each day can help you to establish a good practice schedule. It's easy to do—just carry an index card like the one shown in Figure 4.3 and mark it whenever you do your one-minute practice. If you're using electronic reminders, you may not need the

> ### My Index Card Record of Breathing Pace and Practice Tally
>
> My pace for breathing when I am practicing: inhale (1, 2, 3, 4, 5) exhale (1, 2, 3, 4, 5, 6, 7) pause (1, 2)
>
> My pace for breathing when I am anxious: inhale (1, 2, 3) exhale (1, 2, 3) pause (1)
>
> My practice tally:
> Mon: IIII IIII IIII
> Tues: IIII IIII
> Wed: IIII IIII IIII I

Figure 4.3 My Index Card Record of Breathing Pace and Practice Tally

paper tally, but one reason to temporarily do paper is that when you use the physical action of marking off the tally, your brain reinforces it, and it will be easier for you to remember to breathe as well as easier to feel pleased with yourself for taking charge of your anxiety.

Other Good Practice Methods

It's easy to forget to practice, so here are a few more ideas to help you remember:

- Since most people have their mobile phones handy all day, it's convenient to use apps for breathing practice. Check out the many apps that can remind you of, guide you in, and help you keep track of breathing practice. Some of the newest ones are listed in the Resources section, but you won't have trouble finding one you like. There are many to choose from.
- Program your computer or mobile to give you a ding or a task reminder at various intervals during the day.
- Plan to breathe at specific times every day, such as at the beginning of a class at school or after you brush your teeth. Connecting one action to the other makes the breathing easier to remember.
- Put colored paper dots in odd places—inside a drawer, on the side of the microwave door, on the inside of a car visor, on the cover of a butter dish, or where you can see it when you lift the lid of your copy or scanner machine. Unexpected places are best, where you do not see it

all day and begin to ignore it. When you see the dot, stop and breathe for a minute.

MAKING DIAPHRAGMATIC BREATHING WORK FOR A PANIC ATTACK

Controlling panic happens in two ways. One is identifying the signals that you are about to panic. If you start breathing that very second, before the panic starts, you can avert the attack. The other is learning to slow and stop panic when it is under way. After practicing diaphragmatic breathing for seven days, pick one time of day when you can predict that you will be uninterrupted for a few minutes. For most people, it works best to pick early morning, late evening, or your lunch break. During this one uninterrupted period, you are going to add *one minute of breathing at a time*.

Begin by setting a timer for two minutes, and when you can breathe for two minutes, set it for three minutes the next time. Learn to sustain diaphragmatic breathing for a minimum of five minutes. (Many relaxation apps allow you to do this.) You need at least five minutes to slow and stop a panic attack that is under way. You may enjoy extending this for 10 minutes. If you breathe for 10 minutes with your attention on your breath, you will have a mindfulness practice that will be powerful enough to calm your mind in a lasting way. Once you can breathe for this long, you've set the stage to breathe for other important purposes, such as for profound relaxation, meditation, and cueing the stress response to turn itself off.

OBSTACLES TO DIAPHRAGMATIC BREATHING

Diaphragmatic breathing is a powerful way to disrupt panic and anxiety, but sometimes people have difficulty learning it. Following are a few common obstacles to diaphragmatic breathing, along with ways of getting around them.

- People with breathing problems such as asthma should consider eliminating the counting altogether—it is an intrinsic demand that raises anxiety. Just eliminate the counting and breathe naturally while thinking a sentence with an even rhythm, such as, "Now I breathe in all that is peace. Now I breathe out all that is not peace." Inhale and exhale at an even pace, with no gulps or gasps. You might try just saying one word as you inhale and one word as you exhale—for example, on the inbreath "strong" and on the outbreath "calm."

- Some people get anxious when they start to breathe deeply. Some are afraid of their breath because they fear they will panic while doing something new, or the act of breathing reminds them of their panic. Try limiting your breathing to a minute at a time, reminding yourself that it's only one minute. When that is completely comfortable, add 30-second intervals. If your anxiety continues, you might want to consult a therapist. Anxiety with breathing is sometimes a problem for people who hold their breath to avoid feeling emotions, and you may need support to face that issue.

- It is very rare for diaphragmatic breathing to have no positive impact on panic reduction, but some people report that breathing doesn't seem to help. Have someone observe how you are breathing, and redo the assessment to see if you are inadvertently resorting to one of those ways of breathing.

- Some people have difficulty concentrating on breathing. The best way to handle this is as follows:
  - Notice that you have been distracted and mentally say to yourself, "Oh. A thought." Just notice, with no judgment against yourself for being distracted. Don't get upset with yourself or impatient with the breathing. Consider thoughts as clouds in the sky, just drifting by. You have no need to stop them, examine them, or be irritated that they're there.
  - Redirect your attention to your breath. Focus on the physical sensation of breathing—the feeling of your lungs expanding, the sensation of feeling your waistband or of how your back shifts against a chair, and so on. Feel the breath move through your nostrils or out of your mouth.
  - Count to measure the pace to help keep your focus on the breath.

BREATHING FOR MINIMAL AROUSAL

Basic diaphragmatic breathing can help you be calm before any situation that makes you tense. Whether you have generalized anxiety or social anxiety, staying calm or calming down after you get tense starts with breathing. A particularly good one-minute breathing method to reduce tension involves lengthening your exhale with

Lengthening the Exhale
to Reduce Tension

1. Inhale to the count of 2. Exhale to the count of 2.
2. Inhale to the count of 2. Exhale to the count of 4.
3. Inhale to the count of 2. Exhale to the count of 6.
4. Inhale to the count of 2. Exhale to the count of 8.
5. Inhale to the count of 2. Exhale to the count of 10.

Figure 4.4 Breathing to Reduce Tension

The 5-Count Energizing Breath

1. Inhale to a quick count of 5.
2. Exhale by huffing your breath out in short bursts to the count of 5 (out in bursts: huh-huh-huh-huh-huh).

Figure 4.5 The 5-Count Energizing Breath

every breath until you reach the limit of exhaling (Figure 4.4). You can hear this on the audio track for breathing to reduce tension.

The five-count energizing breath (Figure 4.5) can help you deal with hectic or upsetting situations from which you can take only a short break—such as between classes at school or during a workday. It's especially useful when you need to blow off some steam. You might want to do it privately because it's hard to do subtly—a good place is in the restroom while you're washing your hands. You can do the inhale while washing your hands and then shake water off with five short shakes on the exhale.

THE S.I.M.P.L.E. PLAN TO PRACTICE BREATHING

Breathing for anxiety management is about as simple as it gets. There is very little to figure out once you can actually do the breath. Just getting yourself to believe it will work is more challenging than actually doing it!

One of the problems with anxiety is that it is consuming and can make remembering what to do to combat it difficult. These breathing techniques are not hard to learn, but you do need to practice them if you want to remember how to do them when you feel anxious. They need to become part of your routine. Look at the sample S.I.M.P.L.E. plan in Figure 4.6 and then create your own.

S.I.M.P.L.E. Plan to Practice Breathing

S: What is the *symptom* or *situation*? *I have panic attacks that scare me.*

I: What is the *impact* on my life? *I am starting to avoid going into big spaces like malls where I am afraid it will be hard to get out quickly.*

M: What *method* am I trying? *I am going to practice diaphragmatic breathing by slowly breathing and saying to myself, "Now I breathe in all that is of peace; now I breathe out all that is not of peace."*

P: Practice plan. *I have set my smartphone alarm to ring three times a day and I will also practice whenever I get into my car.*

L: Lifework. *I plan to use this breath when I am in business meetings because the pace and contentiousness are very panic-inducing.*

E: Evaluate. *I will wait and observe after 2 weeks if I feel calmer and perhaps have eliminated panic at work.*

Figure 4.6 S.I.M.P.L.E. Plan to Practice Breathing

S.I.M.P.L.E. Plan to Practice Breathing

S: What is the *symptom* or *situation*? _____

_____

_____

I: What is the impact on my life? _____

_____

_____

M: What *method* am I trying? _____

_____

The 10 Best-Ever Anxiety Management Techniques Workbook

P: *Practice* plan. _____

_____

_____

L: *Lifework.* _____

_____

_____

E: *Evaluate.* _____

_____

_____

THE S.I.M.P.L.E. PLAN TO REDUCE TENSION

Breathing is connected to being able to relax your body. People with generalized anxiety often suffer from physical tension of many varieties, from jaw tightening to lower back pain. If you have social anxiety, staying calm and collected in situations that might have previously made you tense is an important goal in reducing your anxiety. Try breathing when you are tense. Look at the sample S.I.M.P.L.E. plan to reduce tension (Figure 4.7) and then create your own.

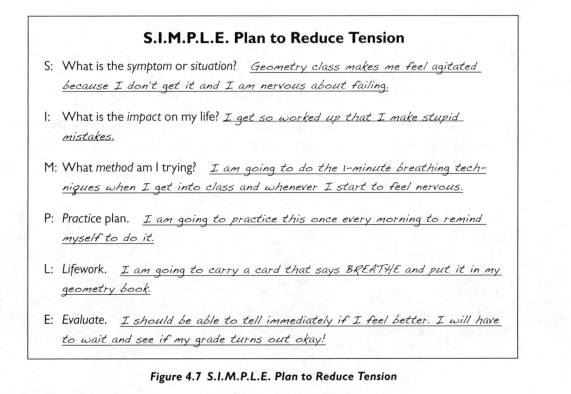

S.I.M.P.L.E. Plan to Reduce Tension

S: What is the *symptom* or *situation?* *Geometry class makes me feel agitated because I don't get it and I am nervous about failing.*

I: What is the *impact* on my life? *I get so worked up that I make stupid mistakes.*

M: What *method* am I trying? *I am going to do the 1-minute breathing techniques when I get into class and whenever I start to feel nervous.*

P: Practice plan. *I am going to practice this once every morning to remind myself to do it.*

L: Lifework. *I am going to carry a card that says BREATHE and put it in my geometry book.*

E: Evaluate. *I should be able to tell immediately if I feel better. I will have to wait and see if my grade turns out okay!*

Figure 4.7 S.I.M.P.L.E. Plan to Reduce Tension

S.I.M.P.L.E. Plan to Reduce Tension

S: What is the *symptom* or *situation*? _____
_____
_____

I: What is the impact on my life? _____
_____
_____

M: What *method* am I trying? _____
_____
_____

P: *Practice* plan. _____
_____
_____

L: *Lifework.* _____
_____
_____

E: *Evaluate.* _____
_____
_____

A FINAL WORD

Breathing methods are an easy, powerful technique to reduce or eliminate physical symptoms of panic and anxiety. Practice until it comes naturally, and you will master physical anxiety for life.

FIVE

Technique #3
Practice Mindfulness

Anxiety, by nature, is focused on what was or what will be. It is rarely focused on the moment. If something bad is happening *right now*, you are probably not *anxious* or *worried* about it—rather, you are probably dealing with it. Of course, this doesn't mean that whatever is happening isn't scaring you—it very well may be—but there's a difference between actively dealing with a situation while you're scared and being anxious or worried about something in the past or future.

Mindfulness is a way of being fully present in the moment you're living in. Such presence is the antithesis of anxiety. Mindfulness as a practice has recently gotten well-deserved attention in the world of anxiety management and has contributed a great deal even since I wrote the first edition of *The 10 Best-Ever Anxiety Management Techniques Workbook*. In this revised edition, I want to add two practices that you can easily do without developing an entire meditation practice: learning to observe and the body scan. These two practices are helpful for diminishing worry about the future and for altering over-attention to panic sensations. Likewise, the practice of mindfulness with shifting attention will help diminish an overfocus on transient, insignificant sensations.

You may have already studied mindful meditation on your own. Applications of mindfulness and meditation are rapidly developing to help people not only with anxiety but also with depression, anger management, and personality disorders, as well as many physical problems, from pain and headaches to cardiovascular problems.

BE MINDFUL OF YOUR OUTER WORLD: LEARN TO OBSERVE

One way to begin being more mindful is to practice observing. A simple way to do this is to think of yourself as a detective who is observing details. The goal is to observe before deciding meaning, just as a detective gathers clues before deciding what theory they may fit. Figure 5.1 suggests how you might be mindful in observing.

You can learn to observe in any setting:

> - Walk outside and observe through your five senses. What do you hear, see, taste, smell and touch?
> - Observe without speaking at the next meeting you attend: How do people speak? Act? Relate to each other? How do they speak to you? Look at you? Remember, no judging about what they are thinking or feeling. Just observe what you see and hear.
> - Watch family members at a family gathering. Watch who says what and observe what others do when a person speaks. Observe the give-and-take, both verbal and nonverbal, without deciding what its meaning is.
> - You may even be able to observe your thoughts as they occur. Just notice the thoughts. Later, you may choose to act or not act on them. You may decide the thought is useful or may even decide your thought is not true or correct.

Figure 5.1 Learn to Observe

BE MINDFUL OF YOUR INNER WORLD: THE BODY SCAN

Even without devoting yourself to a life change in the direction of mindfulness, there is a mindfulness exercise that can bring immediate benefit to those who worry excessively about what is happening in their bodies. This exercise, the body scan meditation, will assist you over time in telling the difference between what is real and what is imagined, and it will help you to ignore fleeting and inconsequential physical sensations.

A starting place for most mindfulness practice is the body scan meditation. This meditation is done lying down and involves developing awareness of each part of your body in a systematic scan from toe to head. The body scan meditation may become the start to your development of a meditation practice. But even if it doesn't, you may have great benefit from it for anxiety relief.

In doing a body scan, at first you sense that your body is you but that *you* are also in some way distinct. When people suffer from panic, social fears, or even worry, they often have the sense that they have no control over their physical sensations and begin to believe that their behavior must be ruled by those sensations. However, body scan meditation ultimately increases your ability to allow sensations to come and go without feeling scared of them. See below table to read how the scan proceeds. You can listen to this from the audio for a guide for the body scan.

Body Scan Meditation

The scan will take about 20 minutes (or longer) and involves the following steps:

1. Lie down comfortably.
2. Allow your breath to slow and deepen.
3. Turn your attention in an interested, open, and loving way to your body, slowly moving through it in the following pattern:
   - Starting with your left foot, attentively scan the toes, the foot, the ankle, the shin and calf, the knee and kneecap, the thigh, the hip.
   - Repeat that awareness with the right leg.
   - Continue from the right hip to awareness of the buttocks and genitals.
   - Move your attention to the abdomen and the lower back.
   - Gradually move your attention up through the torso, the middle back, and the stomach.
   - Note the chest, the heart, the lungs, and then the upper back.
   - Bring your attention to the shoulders.
   - Slowly, allow your attention to focus on each arm, fingers first, then the hand, wrist, forearm, elbow, and upper arm. Then return to the shoulders.
   - Then scan upward through the neck, the throat, the jaw and face and scalp.
   - Breathe.

This body scan may result in surprising awareness of sensations that you had not attended to. It may result in brief intensifying of sensations, and those often pass as you recognize the. I learned early in my career that if you notice sensations, they pass—what an important message for people with anxiety! Your mind-body awareness helps you know how you are being affected by stress, by interaction with others, and even by your own thoughts.

ASSESS YOUR FOCUS ON BODILY SENSATIONS

People with panic disorder are highly vigilant to the physical signs of panic starting—increased heart rate, increased respiration, and so on. People with social anxiety are similarly attuned to physical sensations. When they begin flushing, sweating, or shaking, they worry that other people will see these physical reactions and judge them negatively. People with generalized anxiety often plunge into worry by focusing on sensations of dread that are really just the byproduct of brain chemistry. Whenever you focus on such sensations, you doom yourself to having the physical reaction you fear.

Do you over focus on your bodily sensations? Look at the pattern shown in Figure 5.2 and see if you recognize yourself.

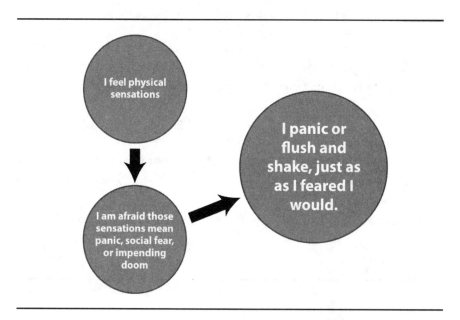

Figure 5.2 Overfocus on Bodily Sensations

The 10 Best-Ever Anxiety Management Techniques Workbook

ASSESS WHETHER YOU TALK YOURSELF INTO FEELING FEAR

Do you talk yourself into feeling fear? Think back to the last time you had a panic attack or were so embarrassed in a social situation that you had to leave. How did you feel, and what did that mean to you? Describe the situation in the following blank diagram (see the sample filled-out diagram in Figure 5.3).

If you find that you can't fill in the diagram, don't worry. The next time you get panicky, feel socially anxious, or feel dread that you turn into worry, pay attention. Ask yourself these questions:

- Did I feel the physical sensations (e.g., dread, panic, queasiness) first?
- Did I worry about whether those sensations would get worse?
- Did they get worse?
- Did I then start to really worry, have a panic attack, or get flushed and sweaty?

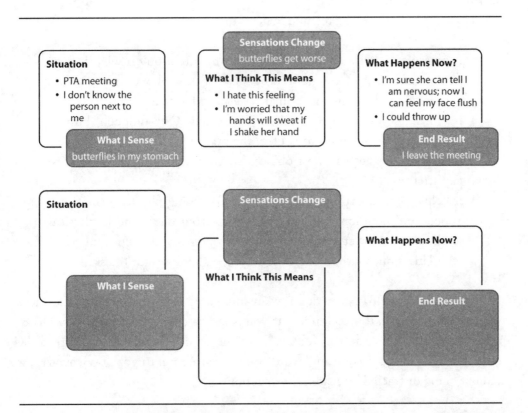

Figure 5.3 Do You Talk Yourself Into Feeling Fear?

If this pattern is familiar to you, you will benefit from the mindfulness technique. You can listen to the track "Mindfulness With Shifting Awareness" on the audio download.

MINDFULNESS WITH SHIFTING AWARENESS

Sara, a client of mine, had developed debilitating panic attacks in adulthood. Diaphragmatic breathing helped her know she wasn't dying while having a panic attack, but she was still afraid of having panic. And she panicked often. She believed every little tingle heralded a panic attack. She created panic out of small, normal changes like a slight chill or a momentary flutter in her stomach. She needed to turn her attention away from physical sensations to what was going on in the world around her—to notice the outer world rather than her inner world. A technique called mindfulness with shifting awareness helped her learn to do that and decreased her panic attacks immediately.

How did it do this? The technique helps in several ways:

- It gives you a sense of control. By focusing attention on what is happening around you, you gain some sense of control over how you are experiencing the moment. You are *choosing* what to attend to.
- It enhances your ability to observe yourself. Our uniquely human capacity to use the brain to control the brain is at the heart of anxiety management, and it is most obvious in your ability to select what to pay attention to.
- It helps you calm yourself by ignoring disturbing physical sensations. When you intentionally turn your focus from one thing (a physical sensation) to another (observations of the outer world), you calm yourself. This is one method of self-soothing—an important life skill.

The audio download provided at www.margaretwehrenberg.com/audiotracks will lead you through this technique. If you prefer not to use the audio download, it will be helpful if you do this for the first time with a partner who can read the script to you. This way, you can devote your full attention to your own awareness without being distracted by reading instructions.

The basic steps are as follows:

1. Sit comfortably with your eyes closed.
2. Be aware of the outside world. What do you notice through your senses (ears, nose, skin)?
3. Shift your awareness back to your body. Notice how it feels as you draw breath into your body, as you inhale through your nose. Notice each sens of inhaling.
4. Notice how it feels to exhale the breath out of your body, exhaling through your nose or mouth. Notice each sensation of exhaling.
5. One more time, shift your awareness to the external world. What do you notice through your senses?
6. Prepare to open your eyes by becoming aware of light coming through your eyelids, and then gradually allow your eyes to open. Bring your attention to the next activity that you are engaging in.

Making It Work for Your Type of Anxiety

Mindfulness with shifting awareness works for panic, social anxiety, and generalized anxiety. Following are a few ideas that might help you make the technique work in various situations and with different types of anxiety.

Mindfulness for Panic Attacks

If you panic, you probably fear having another attack. Mastering this technique will be a big help in getting you to stop:

- Fearing frequent panic attacks
- Fearing "out of the blue" attacks
- Fearing that your panic will worsen if you ignore symptoms of panic
- Fearing new situations in which you might panic

When you have panic disorder, physical sensations may trigger worry that an attack is headed your way. This leads you to escape whatever you're doing at that moment—and when you try to reenter that situation, your brain will watch out for panic. By using this technique to focus on the external world, you can avoid triggering your own panic.

If you have the occasional "out of the blue" attack, use the technique to immediately breathe and shift your focus away from physical sensations. This will ward it off.

If you feel a panic attack coming on before you are fully practiced in breathing or mindfulness, the attack may in fact develop. But don't despair! With practice (and after learning the cognitive techniques in Part III), you will eventually get a handle on managing your panic. Until then, remember that you don't need to be afraid of panic happening—it won't last long, and although it's unpleasant, it's not lethal.

Mindfulness for Social Anxiety

Let's get this on the table: other people *do* notice if you're red in the face, sweating, or shaky. But you must know this also: they don't care! (That is, once you're out of junior high school.) The awfulness of social anxiety symptoms depends on what you tell yourself about them.

Cognitive and behavioral techniques (covered in Parts III and IV) are especially effective in managing social anxiety. But warding off the physical symptoms of anxiety that others notice—small signs of flushing, sweating, or shaking—is a critical component of reducing attacks of nervousness. Mindfulness with shifting awareness can take you:

- Inward (staying focused on breathing rather than on the surrounding hubbub can help you avoid the overstimulation that triggers blushing, sweating, or flushing)
- Outward (by not overfocusing on whether you're showing nervousness, you make yourself care about it less, which reduces the likelihood that you will get seriously flushed or shaky)

Symptoms of social anxiety—that embarrassed, flustered look and feeling—are harder to interrupt than panic, in part due to the fact that others *do* notice these symptoms. Ultimately, if you stop caring whether you flush, you diminish your tendency to do so, but the best way to keep these symptoms at bay is to stay calm in situations that could provoke anxiety about being observed. Mindfulness will do that for you.

Mindfulness for Generalized Anxiety

Because you can do this technique in any setting without being obvious—as long as you simply keep your eyes downcast and not closed—it is a terrific tool for pulling your mind away from worry and directing it to the present moment. As mentioned earlier, the antithesis of worry is to be in the moment and not in the future or past. Because generalized worry occurs anywhere for any reason, this "do it anywhere" technique is terrific for those of you who fret.

The S.I.M.P.L.E. Plan for Practicing Mindfulness With Shifting Awareness

Like diaphragmatic breathing, mindfulness with shifting awareness requires practice so that it comes easily when you need it most. Your assignment: Print the instructions in Figure 5.4 on an index card or make a note of them on your mobile device, then make a S.I.M.P.L.E. plan to use them and carry them with you to remind yourself to try this technique.

Mindfulness with Shifting Awareness

1. Close your eyes and breathe, being fully aware of what your body feels when you breathe.
2. While keeping your eyes closed or downcast, shift your awareness to what you hear, smell, and sense on your skin.
3. Repeat these two steps several times.

Figure 5.4 Mindfulness With Shifting Awareness Instructions

A FINAL WORD

Mindfulness is not a panacea for every aspect of anxiety, but learning to be mindful goes a long way to reducing symptoms of anxiety, whether they are the physical arousal or mental fretting that are so troubling. Learning to observe before forming conclusions, learning to note physical arousal without making it catastrophic, and learning to shift attention from the inner to the outer world as necessary are all aspects of mindfulness that can help you manage anxiety. Mindfulness practices are core tools for controlling all types of anxiety, not to mention the basis of learning to live peacefully with yourself and others.

S.I.M.P.L.E. Plan to Practice Mindlfulness With Shifting Awareness

S: What is the *symptom* or *situation*? _____

_____

_____

I: What is the impact on my life? _____

_____

_____

M: What *method* am I trying? _____

_____

_____

P: *Practice* plan. _____

_____

_____

L: *Lifework.*_____

_____

_____

E: *Evaluate.* _____

_____

_____

SIX

Technique #4
Rest and Relax

Rest and relaxation are not necessarily the same, but lack of rest makes it hard to be relaxed, and sleeping is difficult if you are not relaxed. A great benefit of knowing how to relax is improvement in your quality of sleep. If you suffer from any type of anxiety, you are experiencing physical signs of that negative physical arousal. People with panic have to deal not only with the attack itself but also with its aftermath, and it may take a long time to calm down. Learning to relax intentionally can help with the discomfort of a panic attack and its aftermath. People with generalized anxiety are likely to be physically tense as well as emotionally uptight. They may have physical conditions that are made worse by tension: headaches, TMJ, digestive problems, and so on. Developing a habit of relaxation practices will help diminish that tension. Those with social anxiety may feel comfortable when there is no risk of being observed, but trying to stay calm while imagining an upcoming distressing situation (like speaking in public) poses a different kind of relaxation problem. Taking charge of the physical experience of anxiety by intentionally relaxing the body helps with those situations as well.

Physical relaxation doesn't come naturally to people suffering anxiety. People with generalized anxiety—the worriers and high-drive people—show tension-related arousal, and they may not notice how they have tightened up in the neck or shoulders, lower back, buttocks, or legs until they have pain somewhere. Tension headaches are born of tense muscles in the head and neck that restrict blood flow or affect nerves. For people who suffer from panic attacks, the mental tension of expecting an attack and watching for signs of it leads to tension in the body. For those with social anxiety, the tension prior to being in a public situation in which they fear they are going to be humiliated can be intense. It causes them to tighten

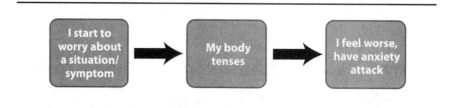

Figure 6.1 Physical Tension Increases Likelihood of Anxiety Attacks

up and be more subject to panic or social anxiety symptoms. Figure 6.1 shows this vicious cycle.

ASSESS YOUR NEED TO RELAX

Every kind of anxiety is stressful. Knowing that you might panic or feel intense social anxiety raises the stress level of your social encounters; being in public settings or doing activities you fear could trigger your symptoms. Stress from work raises anxiety levels. Regardless of the source of your anxiety, your body reacts. You produce more adrenaline and cortisol and have an increased heart rate, blood pressure, and muscle tension. Digestive processes change; you may feel nausea, have increased urgency of urination, or have diarrhea.

Each of the three major types of anxiety addressed in this workbook—panic, generalized anxiety, and social anxiety—has hallmark signs of tension or physical arousal. Check the following lists to see what physical indicators you have. If you suffer from more than one kind of anxiety, you may check symptoms in two or all three categories.

Do You Have These Symptoms?

Do you have any of the following symptoms of panic?

- ☐ Rapid heart rate
- ☐ Shallow breathing
- ☐ Digestive upset
- ☐ Sweating
- ☐ Shakiness, trembling
- ☐ Dizziness
- ☐ Exhaustion when the attack subsides
- ☐ Feelings of tingling or agitation long after the attack subsides

Do you have any of the following symptoms of generalized anxiety?

- ☐ Abdominal pain (this symptom of anxiety is often reported by children)
- ☐ Chest pain
- ☐ Dry mouth or difficulty swallowing
- ☐ Headaches
- ☐ Muscle tension (neck, upper back, lower back)
- ☐ Holding your breath
- ☐ Muscle weakness
- ☐ Fatigue
- ☐ Trouble concentrating
- ☐ Restless sleep

Do you have any of the following symptoms of social anxiety?

- ☐ Blushing
- ☐ Sweating
- ☐ Heart palpitations
- ☐ Shaking hands or knees
- ☐ Quivering voice
- ☐ Nausea

All of these symptoms are related to your body being in a state of arousal. Relaxation, done deliberately, can avert or alleviate these symptoms.

TENSE-AND-RELEASE PROGRESSIVE MUSCLE RELAXATION

Progressive muscle relaxation for tension release is a "first-line" treatment for the physical tension of the anxious body. When combined with slow, deep breathing, this intentional relaxation of muscles helps the parasympathetic nervous system lower blood pressure and slow heart rate and respiration. This technique not only eliminates tension-related stiffness and aches but also lowers arousal levels, which makes triggering anxious physical symptoms more difficult.

The tense-and-release progressive muscle relaxation is provided as an audio download at margaretwehrenberg.com/audiotracks. If you'd rather not use the audio download, you can follow the steps below.

The muscle relaxation will take 10 to 15 minutes. The basic gist of it is to relax all muscle groups in a systematic manner, as follows:

1. Tighten and then release each muscle group—slowly progressing from head to toe—three times before going to the next muscle group.
2. Follow this order: head, neck, shoulders, arms, hands/fingers, chest, abdomen, hips, thighs, shins/calves, ankles, feet/toes.
3. Before moving from one group to the next, feel warmth flood into that muscle group.
4. End with feeling how your feet are connected to the ground.

Muscle Relaxation With Children and Elderly Adults

Because this technique can be done seated or lying down, there is no reason that older adults can't do it. If tensing your muscles feels uncomfortable, however, you can substitute stretching in place of it. Stretching follows the same procedure as tense-and-release relaxation but uses stretching instead of tightening. It is the preferable method for people with sore muscles, arthritis, or connective tissue disorders. As with all exercises, follow the commonsense rule: never do anything that hurts! Sometimes stretching out tense muscles can feel a bit achy, but it should be more like a "good soreness" than outright pain.

Children may not experience the same muscle tension from anxiety, but they do suffer from problems with digestion. Relaxation training can help with that. Doing a physical relaxation is especially useful when children don't cognitively recognize their stress or anxiety. Depending on the child's age, you can improve attention and cooperation by making stretching and relaxing into a game. It can be fun for smaller children to stretch out using images of animals they can relate to (e.g., "Stretch your arms and back like a cat stretching out in the sun," or, "Stretch your face like a lion opening its mouth to yawn"). In a classroom setting, stretching as a group exercise can help children and adolescents relax before things that would make anyone uptight, like taking a test. By having the whole classroom participate, you don't single out any one child, decreasing his or her anxiety about being noticed.

SPHERE-OF-LIGHT IMAGERY FOR RELAXATION

Imagery for muscle relaxation works very well for many, and you can do it even if you have physical restrictions. It requires less time than tense-and-release progressive muscle relaxation. This "sphere-of-light" technique works to relax your whole body, and it is great for people who enjoy imagery. You can use the audio download or follow the steps below. Following is a brief description of the technique:

1. Imagine a glowing sphere of light above your head. Vibrant with warmth and energy, it is the color you associate with peace or calm.
2. Inhale the light through the top of your head.
3. Exhale the warmth of the light down through your body, from the top of your head through every part until you reach your feet.
4. Notice the progress of warm, vibrant energy through each muscle group.
5. Associate a particular word with this sensation, and if you feel tense at any time later in the day, just take a breath, say the word, remember the sensation, and become immediately relaxed.

ONE-BREATH ("CUED") MUSCLE RELAXATION

Once you have learned diaphragmatic breathing and progressive muscle relaxation, you can pair them to produce "cued relaxation." This is a way to relax physically and mentally with one breath. Doing it several times every day can greatly reduce the impact of muscle tension. It also helps you when you sense you're about to panic or when you are in situations that make you tense. If you have social anxiety and are in a situation that raises your tension, this is a subtle way to calm down.

Creating Cued Relaxation

Use the following steps to pair diaphragmatic breathing with muscle relaxation.

1. Several times a day, take a deep, diaphragmatic breath, recalling the way you feel when you are deeply relaxed.
2. Use an image that represents letting tension go—such as plugging your feet into the earth—and as you exhale, send negative energy out of your body and let relaxation flow in behind it throughout the whole body. (Another good image is to send roots from your feet into the earth to draw calm in, and send tension off into the atmosphere.)
3. Accompany a slow, deep breath in with a calming statement, such as "Now I am breathing in all that is of peace. Now I am breathing out all that is not of peace." Whether using an image or a phrase, draw peaceful relaxation inward as you inhale, and exhale the negative energy.
4. When you exhale, send the energy off or out in the way you have imagined it. Note how the muscles from your scalp to your toes let go of tension. Repeat this many times a day.

Figure 6.2 Creating Cued Relaxation

As you get comfortable with this pairing, you will be able to take one breath and feel all your muscles release. In this way, you *cue* muscle relaxation on demand—anywhere, anytime—without anyone noticing.

THE S.I.M.P.L.E. PLAN FOR MUSCLE RELAXATION

Create a S.I.M.P.L.E. plan for muscle relaxation so that you can hold yourself accountable for learning it. Figure 6.3 shows a sample S.I.M.P.L.E. plan; a blank one appears after that for you to fill out.

EXERCISE TO RELAX

You don't have to sit still to relieve your anxiety and tension. In fact, movement may be exactly what you need.

S.I.M.P.L.E. Plan for Muscle Relaxation

S: What is the *situation or symptom*? *I am tense at work, especially when sitting at the computer all day. I tend to clench my teeth while I work, worrying about my job.*

I: What is the *impact* on my life? *I have headaches from this and my neck gets tight.*

M: What *method* am I trying? *I will do daily cued relaxation at least 5 times per workday.*

P: Practice plan. *I will make sure I know diaphragmatic breathing and progressive muscle relaxation. I have done them before, but I will try them several times to be sure I remember them correctly.*

L: Lifework. *I will set my task manager to cue me once per hour to do cued relaxation.*

E: Evaluate. *I will notice in 1 week if I feel less neck tension or have fewer headaches.*

Figure 6.3 S.I.M.P.L.E. Plan for Muscle Relaxation

A stunning amount of research demonstrates the many ways exercise is good for your mind and body. For the high-energy person with lots of muscle tension, physical activities are a better way of relaxing than sitting still is, but exercise can help people with *all* kinds of anxiety. Exercise:

- Promotes healthy brain activity by increasing blood flow
- Keeps the body healthy and able to respond effectively to stress
- Improves self-efficacy—a feeling often diminished when feeling stress

This section will help you get started on exercise. See the Resources section for other ideas.

S.I.M.P.L.E. Plan for Muscle Relaxation

S: What is the *symptom* or *situation*? _____
_____
_____

I: What is the impact on my life? _____
_____
_____

M: What *method* am I trying? _____
_____
_____

P: *Practice* plan. _____
_____
_____

L: *Lifework.* _____
_____
_____

E: *Evaluate.* _____
_____
_____

Getting Started With Exercise

Of all the forms of exercise, aerobic exercise is best for anxiety because it is both a long-term relaxer and a short-term tension releaser. But if you don't yet have an exercise routine, starting at that pace may be too difficult. It's fine to build slowly, doing things you might actually enjoy, so that you have a good chance of staying with it.

The biggest problem may be getting started, so starting small is best. Make a commitment to do one or two small exercise increases. You might begin by committing to walk the dog for an extra block or five extra minutes, or get off the bus one stop before you have to, or walk around the block once whenever you check the

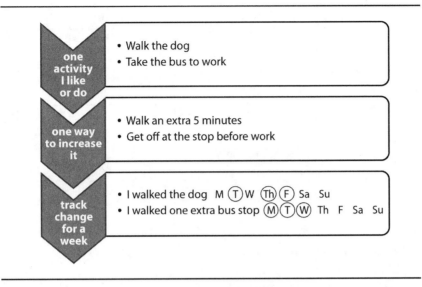

Figure 6.4 Plan to Increase Exercise

mail. It is important to specifically decide on a small step and make a commitment to do it. Figure 6.4 shows an example of a plan to increase exercise; a blank one for you to fill out is offered after it.

If you want to build up to 25 to 45 minutes of aerobic activity, start by asking yourself these questions:

	Day 1	Day 2	Day 3	Day 4	Day 5	Day 6	Day 7
Type of exercise: _____ Duration: _____							
Type of exercise: _____ Duration: _____							

Figure 6.5 Exercise Record

1. What physical things do I like to do?
2. What are my opportunities to do it?
3. Is there anyone who would do it with me?
4. What is the largest possible step I can take in the direction of exercise? (Your weekly goal should be to do a little more each week, until you have achieved the goal of 25 to 45 minutes of aerobic exercise at 70% of your maximum heart rate.)
5. How will I be accountable?

One way to be accountable is to use a simple record-keeping method like the one in Figure 6.5. You can draw the chart on an index card and use it to help you keep track. This is another arena where apps for your cell phone have good tracking options.

SLOW DOWN AND REST

Some people find it very challenging to start an exercise routine. All is not lost. There are other ways to diminish the impact of stress and relax tension. Research about what your brain does while it is "resting" indicates that it is anything but. The downtime of not thinking or doing allows your brain to do the important work of understanding yourself and others, of integrating information, and of "connecting the dots" that it can't do while you are busily thinking on purpose. You may feel anxious about resting your mind and body, as described in the activities in Figure 6.6. You may start thinking you're being lazy or unproductive, but

Figure 6.6 Relaxing Activities

just remember: you will be sharper, remember more, and focus better if you take some downtime. Tension and anxiety take a toll on your productiveness as well, so if you are less tense, you'll be more efficient and (happier) while you work.

Your assignment: Slow down by deciding to do one of these relaxing activities and committing to it.

"I will make a commitment to do _____ by this date _____."

STRETCH TO RELAX

Stretching is useful because you can do it anywhere, anytime (see Figure 6.7). Several of these stretches can be done while you're at work or school or sitting in any confined place, such as a car or airplane seat. They take no time to speak of, requiring you only to pause in whatever activity you're doing. You can stretch while thinking about the next question on a test, while you wait on hold on a phone call, or as your computer prints a document. Although one 15-second stretch is sufficient

Quick Stretches That Can Be Done Anywhere

- *Yawn-and-stretch.* Simply yawn, stretch your arms upward, and release. Repeat.

- *Torso relaxation.* For gentle back stretching, try torso relaxation. Standing with your feet comfortably spread apart for support, let your head fall forward, leading the torso down and bending at the waist. Return to an upright position by reversing the motion. Continue the action of this simple stretch into an overhead stretch once you are upright. Lift up your arms, reaching high overhead, and gently tilt your head by lifting your chin until you gaze directly up. Make this and all releases gentle.

- *Leg lunges.* If you get up to walk somewhere, pause for a moment and do gentle leg lunges. This is great when you have been sitting too long or are too tight.

- *Calf stretch.* If you have the opportunity to go up or down a few stairs, pause, hold the handrail, and with your toes balanced on the edge of the stair, let your heel drop, thereby stretching the back of your leg. Do this for 2 seconds of stretch and then pause. Repeat it a few times. You can do this one leg at a time with the other foot firmly planted on the stair so you don't have to worry about balance.

- *Head tilt.* Tilt your head so that your ear falls toward your shoulder as far as it can without hurting. Then raise your head upright. Let your chin drop slowly to your chest, feel the stretch down your back, and then raise your head upright. Drop the other ear toward your shoulder and, again, raise your head upright. Let your head feel heavy and drop slowly backward. Return to an upright position before you repeat this. *Do not rotate your neck in a circle.* You can do this while seated at your desk, even as you talk on the phone or look at the computer, without losing any time from work.

- *Arm stretch.* Raise one arm straight overhead and then bend it at the elbow, reaching with that hand down as if you were going to scratch between your shoulder blades. Then relax. With the same arm, reach across your chest and wrap your hand around the opposite shoulder. Using the unoccupied hand, grasp the elbow of the reaching arm and gently exert pressure to increase the stretch in the shoulder and upper arm. Again, you can do this while seated at your desk without interrupting work time.

The 10 Best-Ever Anxiety Management Techniques Workbook

Quick Stretches That Can Be Done Anywhere

- *Seated posture change.* You can prevent the tightening up that occurs when seated at a desk using the seated posture change. This preventive measure can be practiced constantly if your job requires sitting all day. It involves regularly rotating through changed positions. Have a small stool (or just a box) by your feet on which to rest them. In the first position, sit with one foot raised. In the next, sit with the other foot raised. Then sit with both raised, and then neither. Hold each position for 15 minutes before rotating to the next. Another version of this exercise is to use a back pillow or rolled towel, and put it first behind your lower back, then your middle back, and then do without it.

Figure 6.7 Quick Stretches That Can Be Done Anywhere

to release a little tension, some stretching experts recommend several 2-second stretches to loosen up, so do what feels best to you. Practicing these stretches will help keep you loose when circumstances could make you uptight.

SLEEP!

It's impossible to be relaxed when you're exhausted. Good sleep underlies good health, including good mental health. When you have anxiety, your sleep suffers for several reasons, depending on the cause of the anxiety. The profound mental relaxation promoted by good rest is not obtainable in any other way. Getting a good night's sleep can often be achieved just by relaxing your body well enough and having the right environment. (Adding the clear-the-mind method from Chapter 9 can also help. It's called "Contain Your Worry" on the audio download.) If that doesn't work, you may need to give your sleep more attention. Check out the section on sleeping in *The 10 Best-Ever Anxiety Management Techniques* for ideas to handle worry dreams, or go to the Resources section of this book for heavy-duty sleep management help. You will find the website of the American Academy of Sleep Management (www.aasmnet.org) to be an excellent source for information that can help you figure out how to get a good night's sleep. Figure 6.8 also gives some suggestions for improving your sleep hygiene.

> ## Improving Your Sleep
>
> *Set a pattern of sufficient sleep*
> - Be regular about the times you sleep.
> - Make enough time for sleep. Go to bed early enough to stay in bed for a full 8 hours, even if you wake sooner than that for a while.
>
> *Make the environment conducive to sleep*
> - Sleep in a room that is as cool and as dark as possible.
> - Screen out environmental noises (like people talking in another room or noise from the street). When the environment has variable noises, like an apartment building, use some form of consistent noise like a fan or white-noise machine.
>
> *Prepare the brain and body for sleep*
> - Eliminate violent or exciting TV for several hours before sleep.
> - Take a warm bath for 20 minutes before sleep.
> - Create a drowsy brain with herbal teas such as catnip or chamomile.
> - Keep caffeine as low as possible, especially after noon, because it is a stimulant.
> - Do not work on email, messages, voicemails, or computer projects close to bedtime. A mind racing with ideas will have trouble dropping off to sleep.
>
> *Plan to handle restless sleep quality*
> - Handle worry dreams by awakening fully for a few minutes and shake the dream off by consciously finishing the topic, dispelling its importance, and then focus on something pleasant while falling back to sleep.
> - Plan for awake times—literally, plan what you will watch, read, or think about if you awaken to avoid slipping into negativity or worry.

Figure 6.8 Improving Your Sleep

THE S.I.M.P.L.E. PLAN TO GET STARTED ON RELAXATION

You may want to try all the relaxation methods suggested in this chapter, or just choose the one or two that appeal to you. Maybe your issue is sleep—not sleeping enough or sleeping too restlessly. Maybe it's just muscle tension that bothers you. Perhaps you want to be more relaxed in meetings or classrooms. Knowing your relaxation goals will help you decide where to start in addressing your particular problem. Figure 6.9 provides a quick look at where to start.

Once you've picked a place to start, fill out a S.I.M.P.L.E. plan to help you follow through on it. You can certainly try more than one method—if you do, photocopy the following blank S.I.M P.L.E. plan and fill out a copy for each method.

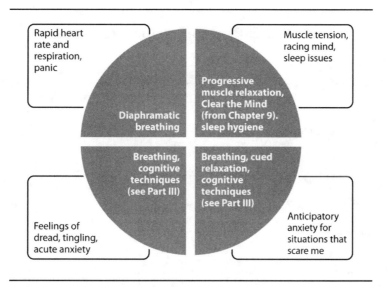

Figure 6.9 Choosing Where to Start

A FINAL WORD

The biggest impediment to using this technique is not believing that relaxation is powerful enough to help when you feel very upset. That may be true when you first start tackling your anxiety, but as you continue to practice this technique, its value will grow. The more you learn to relax your body, the greater the benefit will be to you.

S.I.M.P.L.E. Plan to Enhance Relaxation

S: What is the *symptom* or *situation*? _____

_____

_____

I: What is the impact on my life? _____

_____

_____

M: What *method* am I trying? _____

_____

_____

P: *Practice* plan. _____

_____

_____

L: *Lifework.* _____

_____

_____

E: *Evaluate.* _____

_____

_____

PART III

Managing Your Anxious Mind

SEVEN

Technique #5 Stop Catastrophizing

Thoughts that begin with the words "Oh, no!" are likely to be followed by thoughts that are "catastrophizing"—that is, thoughts that make the worst of whatever you are about to experience. When you catastrophize, you make a mountain out of a molehill, expecting things to be "awful" or "terrible" or "the worst possible outcome."

Catastrophizing is common in all three types of anxiety—panic, social anxiety, and generalized anxiety. People who suffer panic or social anxiety tend to catastrophize both their symptoms and the outcome of their symptoms. They live in fear of having the strong negative feelings of a panic attack or of the possibility that they will blush, sweat, or shake in a social situation. People who have panic attacks often believe they are dying, going crazy, or losing control. And people with social anxiety are convinced that they will certainly be rejected or feel humiliated and see this as the worst possible feeling they could ever imagine.

When people with generalized anxiety feel that familiar sensation of dread coming on, they go on "scan mode" to see what could be causing it, usually assuming the sensation is due to more than just a glitch in their anxious brain. They will find something wrong in their life to explain the dread, which makes them feel even worse because now they believe, "Yes! Something *is* wrong." Figure 7.1 shows an example of how this can happen.

When you suffer from anxiety, your body—for no good reason other than neurochemistry—generates sensations that feel like anxiety. And the emotional

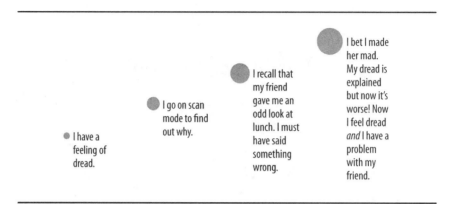

Figure 7.1 Going on Scan Mode to "Catastrophize" Dread Sensation

part of your brain, geared to protect you against bad things happening, reacts to these physical signals *as if they are the truth*. Convinced that if you're feeling physical symptoms of anxiety, there must indeed be something very real to worry about, the emotional part of your brain catastrophizes the sensations. And it's hard to disbelieve your own brain telling you something bad is about to happen! That's why you need to make deliberate decisions to identify and divert those thoughts.

ASSESS YOUR CATASTROPHIZING

If you catastrophize, you will see yourself in one of the following examples. Figure 7.2 illustrates an example of catastrophizing in panic disorder, Figure 7.3 shows it with generalized anxiety and Figure 7.4 shows it with social anxiety. Following each of these figures is a blank one where you can write in your own physical symptoms and the thought process that follows them.

If you see yourself in any of these three examples, read on to learn how to interrupt and defeat catastrophic thinking.

LOGIC VERSUS EMOTION

It's true that the physical symptoms of anxiety are highly unpleasant—so unpleasant, in fact, that when they appear, the emotional part of your brain assumes a catastrophe must be happening:

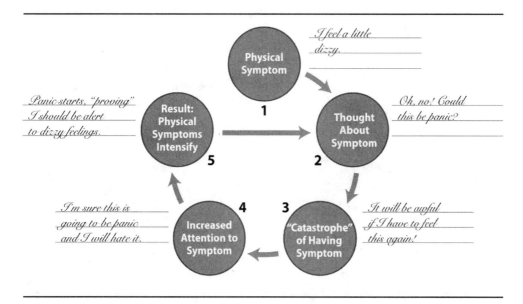

I feel a little dizzy. — Physical Symptom (1)

Oh, no! Could this be panic? — Thought About Symptom (2)

It will be awful if I have to feel this again! — "Catastrophe" of Having Symptom (3)

I'm sure this is going to be panic and I will hate it. — Increased Attention to Symptom (4)

Panic starts, "proving" I should be alert to dizzy feelings. — Result: Physical Symptoms Intensify (5)

Figure 7.2 Panic Disorder Catastrophizing

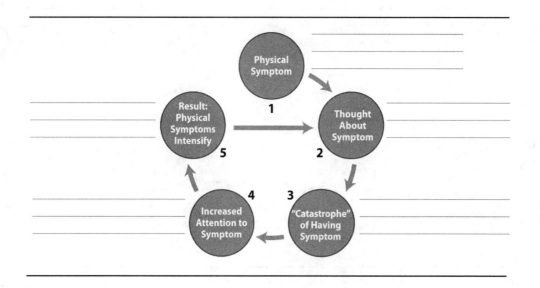

- If you panic fairly often, your brain is sensitized and primed for the next attack. You may believe that you can't control your panic and become terrified when you even *think* about panicking.
- If you have generalized anxiety, your brain goes into "Oh, no!" mode when some situation sparks a worry. This triggers a stab of adrenaline,

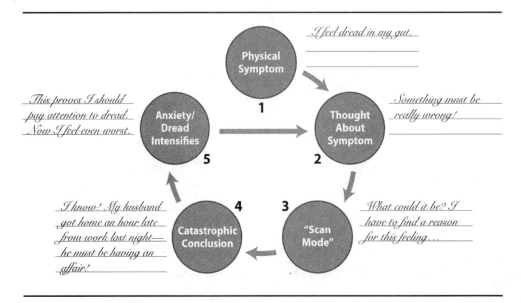

I feel dread in my gut.

Something must be really wrong!

What could it be? I have to find a reason for this feeling...

I know! My husband got home an hour late from work last night—he must be having an affair!

This proves I should pay attention to dread. Now I feel even worst.

Figure 7.3 Generalized Anxiety Catastrophizing

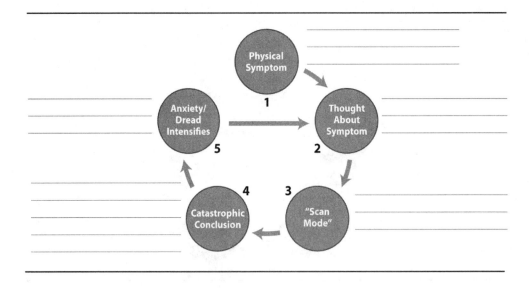

which causes the sensation of stomach-sinking fear. So, even if the initial mistake or problem that caused the worry is minor, your skyrocketing anxiety about it makes you believe it's a catastrophe that may not have a reasonable solution.

The 10 Best-Ever Anxiety Management Techniques Workbook

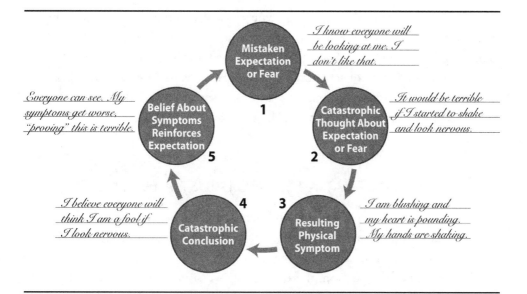

I know everyone will be looking at me. I don't like that.

It would be terrible if I started to shake and look nervous.

I am blushing and my heart is pounding. My hands are shaking.

I believe everyone will think I am a fool if I look nervous.

Everyone can see. My symptoms get worse, "proving" this is terrible.

Figure 7.4 Social Anxiety Catastrophizing

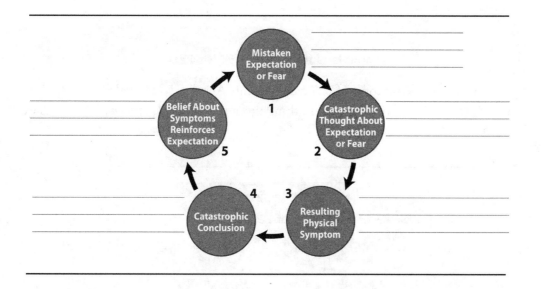

- If you are burdened with social anxiety, you have a brain structure that is more sensitive to feelings of anxiety—those sensations feel worse to you than they feel to other people. You are also overly alert to negative faces, seeing more rejection than is really there.

To defeat catastrophic thinking, you must use deliberate, emphatic logic to override that emotional voice telling you your symptoms are awful or a sign of something bad. In other words, you must use the logical part of your brain to override the emotional part of your brain to say, "Hey, wait! I know you think something very bad is happening, but let's stop for a second to see if that's really true." The following methods will help you do just that.

LEARN THAT A FEELING IS JUST A FEELING

There is a four-step process to help you learn that a feeling is just a feeling and interfere with catastrophic thinking no matter which kind of symptom you're experiencing. This process is described in Figure 7.5.

At the end of this section, there is a blank version of this figure that will help you tailor this four-step process to your own specific symptoms. Before you fill it out, look at the following material on how this technique applies to the three main types of anxiety.

Panic Is Unpleasant but Not Lethal

Are the physical symptoms of panic unpleasant? Absolutely. Unwelcome? Yes. Distracting? No doubt. But they are nothing more than that! *They won't kill you.* They

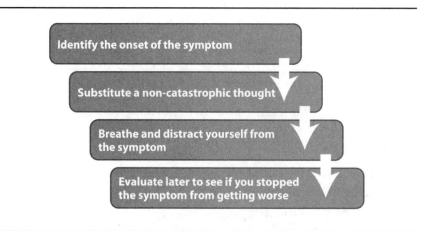

Figure 7.5 Learn That a Feeling Is Just a Feeling

The 10 Best-Ever Anxiety Management Techniques Workbook

are just sensations. Ask yourself, "Have I survived every panic attack?" (If you are reading this, the only answer is yes!)

If you suffer from panic, here are some guidelines for filling out the blank "a feeling is just a feeling" diagram.

1. Identify the symptom that gets you on the catastrophic thinking track.
2. Write down the catastrophic thoughts you most often have and substitute them with the corrective thought. For example, you might substitute "If I panic, it will be awful" with "Panic is unpleasant—but it isn't lethal."
3. Select which breathing method you prefer (see Chapter 4) and a method to distract yourself. For example, you might decide to look at pictures of your last vacation or pat your dog for a minute.
4. Evaluate how this worked. This step helps your brain fight the catastrophic thinking next time.

Coming to believe that "a feeling is just a feeling" requires paying attention to outcomes. Even a full-fledged, extremely unpleasant panic attack is eventually going to stop and leave you unharmed. Noticing the outcome—that an attack was brief and you survived it—and noticing that you suffer less when you don't catastrophize are vital to increasing your confidence that you can stop panic.

Dread Is Just a Feeling That Can Occur Even When Nothing Is Wrong

When else is a feeling just a feeling? High-drive people with generalized anxiety are biologically set up to get a gut feeling that is a lot like the feeling you get when something is about to go wrong—that "uh-oh" feeling of dread. That queasy gut is a signal to look out for something, but it is not an *urgent* feeling, like danger.

To escape catastrophizing, you must believe this: that feeling doesn't mean anything. Many people want to believe the dread *must* mean something and fight against distracting themselves from it. They ask, "But what if something really is wrong and I ignore it?" The trick is to ask yourself if the dread *preceded* your awareness that something might be wrong. If the answer is, "Yes, I noticed the dread first and then tried to figure it out," you can reasonably assume that there's no good reason for your feelings of worry, and you can proceed to distract yourself from that miserable feeling without figuring it out. (For a longer discussion of the biological basis of dread and some caveats to knowing it is just a feeling without meaning, see my books *The Anxious Brain* and *The 10 Best-Ever Anxiety Management Techniques*.)

If you suffer from generalized anxiety, here are some guidelines for filling out the blank "a feeling is just a feeling" diagram at the end of this section.

1. When you get the "uh-oh" feeling of dread, ask yourself how you feel it in your body.
2. Stop catastrophizing about this feeling. Substitute a statement such as, "Dread is just a feeling that can occur even when nothing is wrong," or, "If I really have a problem, I won't have to go looking for it."
3. Choose a breathing technique that you like (see Chapter 4) and immediately distract yourself, perhaps by one of the thought replacements in Chapter 8, such as thinking about the work you are doing right at this moment.
4. Evaluate later, noticing that the feeling went away and there was no problem causing it.

Embarrassment Is Just a Feeling

The flushing, trembling, sweaty feelings that seem to happen whenever you are in public are very hard to control. To stop catastrophizing about those feelings, you must do two things: first, dispute what you believe will happen if others notice your nervousness, and then ignore your sensations.

It is true that your signs of anxiety are visible to others. What is *not true* is that others will reject you because you look nervous. Dispute your belief that you will be humiliated or rejected by telling yourself, "Being noticed is not the same thing as being rejected."

Interactions between adolescents are an exception to this. Teenagers are often unkind to each other, and they may indeed make a big deal out of you flushing or sweating. If you are an adolescent, the key to stopping catastrophizing is learning to shrug off the appearance of anxiety. Learning, practicing, and using words and actions that show you are unconcerned—like laughing with peers about your tendency to blush—is a good way to deal with the runaway thoughts of social anxiety. If you need help finding good ways to shrug off the symptoms, ask a parent, trusted teacher, or school therapist.

Once you have disputed your assumptions about what will happen, it becomes much easier to simply ignore your flushing, shaking, or sweating. You can decide it would *not be awful* if that should happen and just live with it, using breathing to stay as calm as possible.

If you suffer from social anxiety, here are some guidelines for filling out the blank "a feeling is just a feeling" diagram.

1. What are your signs of embarrassment? For example, do you get red in the face, feel a bit nauseous, or find that your voice quivers?
2. Stop catastrophizing about this feeling. Note what you normally say to yourself—such as, "It will be awful if they notice I'm sweating"—and substitute that statement with, "Being noticed is not the same as being rejected."
3. Choose a breathing technique that you like (see Chapter 4) and immediately distract yourself, perhaps by noticing all the decorations in the room.
4. Evaluate later: Did your feeling subside? Were you indeed rejected? Did you have some success in doing some of the social activity without symptoms?

Here is the blank "a feeling is just a feeling" diagram for you to fill out.

What are your symptoms?

What do you normally tell yourself, and what would you prefer to think?

What type of breathing and distraction will you do?

Evaluate: How did that work?

DEBUNK THOUGHTS ABOUT DYING, GOING CRAZY, OR LOSING CONTROL

This method works especially well with panic, although it can be adapted to deal with other types of anxiety as well. People who suffer from panic are especially prone to catastrophizing because the sensations are so intense. "I'm dying!" "I'm going crazy!" "I'm losing control!" Although the logical part of your brain knows that you have survived other panic attacks without these consequences, your emotional brain still goes there. And the strength of its belief is powerful. I once had a client who had a panic attack relapse after many months of getting better at preventing them. Even though his logical brain was saying, "It's probably just panic," his emotional brain told him, "But *this* time it could be a heart attack." It was only after a visit to the emergency room and thousands of dollars of medical tests that his emotional brain finally believed his logical brain.

The following two steps will help you override your emotional brain:

1. Tell yourself you have always survived panic.
2. Watch how breathing slows you down and remind yourself that you know how to stop panic, even when it's uncomfortable.

Search for the Exact Image or Thought

Get specific about what you are envisioning when you say to yourself, "I am dying!" or "I am going crazy!" or "I am losing control!" and then begin a process of asking, "What happens next?" until you can't go any further. This method is not intended to make you feel worse; the key is going through the thought to the other side.

For example, let's look at the catastrophizing statement "I am dying." Find an exact image—the one you play in your mind like a movie—of what you really fear: collapsing in the street, being taken to the emergency room, and so on. (It's not unusual for people to find that, despite their fear of dying, they don't have any specific image of what would happen if they *were* dying.) So, let's say you imagine yourself collapsing. Now ask yourself, "What happens next?" (Asking this question is very important, so if you find you can't do it alone, have someone help by asking you the question, repeatedly, in a gentle way.) The next step might be, "They hook me up to machines," or, "My chest hurts more," or, "I am blacking out." Keep on asking, "Then what happens?" until you get to, "Then I die." *Then, ask yourself again:* "What happens next?" You would not be alone if you laughed when you realized that the panic would at least be over. But there's a good chance that you will understand more about what the panic means to you or what fear leads you to believe you are dying.

I do want to acknowledge that for some people, the fear of dying is real and raw. The idea that panic is killing them is not real, but fear of death is, and I intend no disrespect to those who suffer from that fear. Fear of dying may underlie health anxiety, which is more of a worry disorder, and I discuss handling that in Chapter 8. But if you find that your fear of dying is real and difficult to tolerate, I strongly suggest you talk with a therapist who is willing to travel with you in that discussion. You might need to address your spiritual beliefs, your view of yourself, and your learnings about death and dying from personal experiences or teachings in childhood. Those areas are too broad for a discussion here, and they are important to work through, but I want to add one thought: you are alive now. Stay in this moment and validate your life by committing to enjoy it as much as possible.

Figure 7.6 shows how this worked for one person who suffered from panic. His worries were about losing his job and running out of money because he had no substantial savings, but his panic focused on fears of dying. My remarks to him are in brackets.

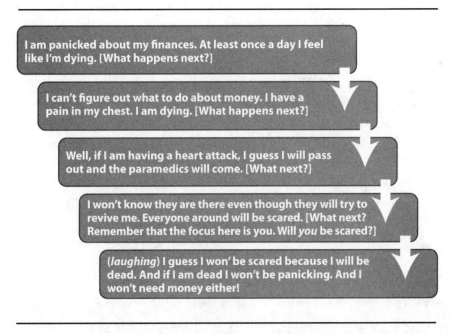

Figure 7.6 One Man's Catastrophe

By pursuing his thoughts all the way through dying, this man was able to see that what he feared was his financial challenge—the catastrophic thought, "I am dying!" was a distraction from (and certainly not a help in) addressing his real problems.

Now let's look at the catastrophizing statement "I am losing control!" If you fear losing control, ask yourself, "If someone were observing me, what exactly would I look like? What would I be doing or saying?" Imagine this in detail. See yourself as if someone else were reporting on your *behavior*, not on your *feelings*. Keep asking the question, every time you describe one action, "Then what?"—all the way through to the end of the panic attack. A typical progression might be something like this: A mother who won't go on a field trip with her daughter because she fears panicking on the bus might imagine herself short of breath, looking wild-eyed. When she asks herself, "Then what?" she might respond with, "I would run off the bus!"—as if that were proof of losing control. When asked the question "Then what?" again, she might feel confused, wondering, "Isn't that enough?" But, pondering it further, she might find a way to get back on the bus or come to the realization that the other parents can manage the field trip without her.

By using this question again and again to walk yourself through to the end of the attack, you may well recognize that your fear of losing control is invalid.

Finally, let's look at the catastrophizing statement "I am going crazy!" Of all the fears, this one is least likely to have a vivid realistic image. Usually people are only aware that some part of them is afraid that panic means they are crazy. But visualizing a specific image helps here, too. Ask yourself, "What does going crazy look like?" Again, run through the image like a movie, pursuing it until the panic is ended, as I've described. When you know what underlies the fear of being crazy, you will know how to resolve that fear and be less likely to catastrophize.

Following is a blank diagram for you to fill out. In the uppermost box, write in your version of the catastrophic exclamation "I am dying, going crazy, or losing control!" (This process also works well for social anxiety, with the catastrophic exclamation being something like "I will be humiliated!") Then, for each of the subsequent boxes, ask yourself, "What happens next?" and write in your answers. This will help you debunk your fears and stop catastrophizing.

Plan to Panic

It's very easy for people to become afraid of the thing they were doing when they felt panic. For example, if you panic while you're driving on a highway in the rain, you are likely to feel afraid of panicking the next time you drive in the rain. Subsequently,

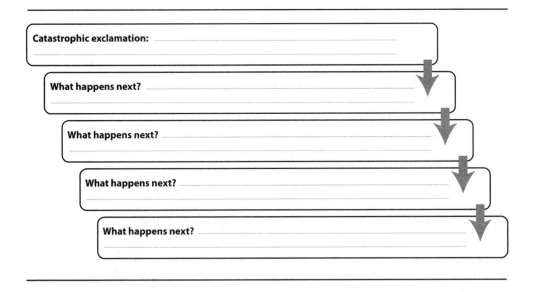

Catastrophic exclamation: _____

What happens next? _____

What happens next? _____

What happens next? _____

What happens next? _____

you might panic not only when you're driving on the highway in the rain, but also any time it rains and any time you're driving no matter how dry the road.

It might seem logical to try to figure out ways to avoid panicking, but this only makes things worse. A better approach is to prepare to panic and plan how to cope with it. It's unlikely that you'll be able to anticipate every potential trigger of panic, so just plan on panicking.

**Preparation involves eight simple steps.
Check these off as you complete them.**

☐ 1. Learn to breathe away panic (Technique #2).

☐ 2. Review each step of the situation that you have been avoiding (Technique #8).

☐ 3. Desensitize every aspect of the situation that you fear could trigger you (Techniques #8 and #10). Note any aspect of the activity that caused you to feel nervous and apply a method to calm down while imagining it. (Systematic desensitization, EMDR, energy therapy, and other methods can help you imagine the aspect of the situation that makes you feel panicky and calm down prior to going into it. See the Resources section for more information on therapy methods for desensitizing.)

☐ 4. Practice. Try a mini-version of the event or activity. For example, plan to get on one short stretch of highway at a time when there is little traffic and

---

you can get off and go back home or continue on to your destination without using the highway. Stop the practice session at the planned time, even if it is going well.

☐ 5. Write down exactly what you will do if and when you panic. Carry your plan with you in your mobile device or on an index card that you always have with you.

☐ 6. Review your plan before you go into the situation, and have it handy so you can grab it should you panic.

☐ 7. Then try it for real, knowing that if you panic, you have a plan.

☐ 8. Evaluate how it went.

    ☐ Commend yourself for handling difficulties.

    ☐ Praise yourself for doing the whole thing without panic.

    ☐ Decide how to amend your plan if you had a problem.

    ☐ Notice that you lived through it no matter how it went.

LEARN TO KNOW (AND CHOOSE TO SHOW) ANGER

Sometimes anger is so anxiety-producing that people don't even recognize that they feel angry about something. For example:

- You might risk being hurt by someone else if you show you are angry.
- You might not know how to show anger without behaving in a way that would bother you. For example, if you tend to yell or swear or speak harshly, you may try to avoid being angry in an attempt to avert these behaviors.
- If you have been hurt, abused, or emotionally rejected in the past, feelings of anger may bring back memories of those experiences, which produce anxiety. Thus, you may decide that it's better not to feel anger.
- If you were raised to believe anger is wrong, bad, or sinful, you may not want to even know you feel anger.
- If you are angry at someone you love or need (such as a spouse or boss), you may rightly fear you will compromise or lose that relationship if you express your anger.

Does any of this sound familiar to you? If it does, then even *feeling* anger may seem like a catastrophe, and denying that you feel angry—even to yourself—becomes a mechanism to stay safe.

What does this have to do with anxiety? Veronica was convinced that anger had nothing to do with her anxiety. Week after week, however, she told me about things that would have made anyone angry. Her husband forgot she needed the car and drove to work instead of taking the train, stranding her at home all day. Her daughter brought her two-year-old twins over for a visit and then asked Veronica to keep them overnight so she could go meet friends. Every time Veronica recounted a situation like this, she explained it away as not being that bad. But as the incidents built up into a pattern, she found herself feeling unappreciated, taken advantage of, and, yes, angry! When it occurred to her that she was angry, her anxiety level immediately dropped.

When you are aware that something is causing anger, you will feel the anger, not the anxiety. You might need time to learn and practice anger management, conflict resolution, negotiating, assertiveness, and other skills that will help you use anger productively in your life, but the first step is recognizing that anger is the feeling you have.

Six Steps for Decatastrophizing Anger

This method is not about showing anger. It is about *knowing* anger. Knowing you are angry is not the same as showing you are angry. The goal is to reduce anxiety by identifying when anxiety masks anger. After becoming aware that anger may be present, you can learn how to handle it.

The method is simple. When you are in the grip of strong sensations of tension, worry, stomach-squeezing doom, and the like—especially when they come on rather suddenly—look for unrecognized anger underneath the anxiety.

Step #1. The next time you feel strong anxiety, immediately sit down and, in single words or brief phrases, write as long a list as possible in answer to this *specific* question: "If I were angry, *what might I be angry about?*" The hypothetical nature of the question is a key feature. You don't have to feel committed to being angry about anything once it's on the list—you are only being speculative about it. Use the following diagram to compile a list of hypothetical things that might anger you. Write ideas in the boxes. These can be things that are big or small, recent or from long ago. You can decide later if it's true that you're angry about any of them.

Step #2. Reflect on what it felt like to write the list. How does it feel to see what you have? What happened to your anxiety level?

Step #3. Review the list. Is there anything on the list that needs action? What can you let go?

Step #4. If something requires action because you are being hurt, taken advantage of, ignored, or worse, talk over your intended action with someone so that you don't put yourself at risk with a badly handled situation. After all, you were feeling your anger as anxiety, so there is a good chance you might not be good at handling anger.

Step #5. Consider skill-building for expressing anger. Learning to be assertive instead of aggressive is a good start for people who are either reluctant or excessive in expressing anger.

Step #6. You can then destroy the list or discuss it in therapy. I ask my clients to discuss with me their reactions to writing this list, and if they feel comfortable it can be helpful for them to share the whole list. When they do review the list and their reactions to writing it, they gain insight into the connection between anger and anxiety. This opens the door to deeper levels of psychotherapy to resolve psychological problems with being angry.

Learn How to Be Angry

Once you know you are angry, you may have to figure out *how* to be angry. If you've had bad experiences with being angry in the past, you may not have gained much practice in appropriately expressing anger. You may either blow up or be too quiet, both of which are ineffective. If you know that you are prone to excessive anger (anxiety can prompt some pretty startling displays of excessive anger), seek some guidance from anger management books to learn to tone down that angry expression. There are also excellent books on assertiveness if you worry that you don't express anger openly enough.

A FINAL WORD

Stopping every sort of catastrophizing will take you a long way in managing your anxious mind. These different ways you immediately go to the "Oh, no!" or "Uh-oh!" in any situation can trigger anxiety—from intense panic to uptight tension. By practicing the methods of this technique, you will be able to sidestep experiences of anxiety before they start or calm them down quickly if they do crop up.

THE S.I.M.P.L.E. PLAN TO STOP CATASTROPHIZING

Your S.I.M.P.L.E. plan is just a way to decide where to start. Using the tools and methods outlined in this chapter, you can begin to lessen every kind of anxiety you feel. Fill in the following plan with your idea of how to identify your catastrophic thinking and then interrupt it. For example, you might plan to listen to the audio track "Stop Catastrophic Thinking" for several days until you feel sure you will remember the replacement thoughts.

S.I.M.P.L.E. Plan to Stop Catastrophizing

S: What is the *symptom* or *situation?* _____

_____

_____

I: What is the impact on my life? _____

_____

_____

M: What *method* am I trying? _____

_____

_____

P: *Practice* plan. _____

_____

_____

L: *Lifework.*_____

_____

_____

E: *Evaluate.* _____

_____

EIGHT

Technique #6

Stop Anxious Thoughts

People experience anxiety because they are set up by biology or life experience to feel anxious even when nothing is objectively wrong. This means that anxiety is a condition looking for content. If you feel anxious, your thoughts start to look around for the reason. Readers with generalized anxiety symptoms know what this feels like, even if they have not previously recognized the searching quality of their anxious thoughts. This process also occurs for people with panic and social anxiety. Any type of anxiety affects thinking. In this chapter, you will engage in healthy, realistic thinking to override the unhealthy, unrealistic thoughts that plague you.

Everyone feels anxiety. It is a normal reaction when you face an ambiguous situation. Anxiety is the emotional and physical state that results when you don't know what is happening, what will happen, or what to do about what is happening. That state of anxious arousal demands resolution. If you are experiencing anxiety, you want to get rid of it—*pronto!* So, what do you do? You move into "what-if" thinking mode. You try to figure out what is happening, what will happen, or what you should do about what is happening. If you can figure it out, your anxiety will diminish.

WHAT-IF THINKING IS A REASONABLE RESPONSE TO ANXIETY

Anxious thoughts become an attempt to get rid of anxiety, because if you can figure out what is going on and what to do about it, the ambiguity is resolved. Then you can take action to solve the problem you figured out. For example, suppose you're having a lot of anxiety about starting college. Your what-if thoughts might be, "What if I can't stand my roommate? What if I can't make friends? What if the workload is too much for me to handle?" These what-if thoughts can be helpful, because there are ways you can address them: You can call the school to get your roommate's contact information and send an email to the person to begin the introduction process. You can look into extracurricular groups you might be able to join to begin to make friends. You can go through the course catalogue and select a group of courses that will give you a balanced workload.

But what if you feel anxiety for no good reason? What if you feel it simply because of your genetic makeup or because ongoing stress has triggered "free-floating" anxiety (anxiety not connected to real-life events)? This is when those what-if thoughts begin to cause trouble. Because there is no *real* problem, you start creating unreasonable what-if scenarios: "What if my husband dies in a car accident?" "What if I lose my job and can't support my family?" These thoughts are your brain's effort to get rid of unpleasant anxiety, but if your husband is not, in fact, in imminent danger of dying in a car accident, and if there isn't any real risk of losing your job, then the what-if thinking does *not* resolve the anxiety—in fact, it makes it worse. Now your thoughts are crowded with *potential* problems that only *might* be issues. And your anxiety gets worse because the what-if thinking has created real ambiguity. You feel bad, you don't know why, and you can't figure it out. This is how what-if thinking increases in a vicious circle.

An anxiety disorder is not an outcome of your thinking, but rather the other way around. Excessive anxious thinking is an outcome of an anxiety disorder. And here is the dilemma. When your anxiety is not a reaction to a real-life scenario, then the ensuing what-if thinking worsens the anxiety. The same process occurs with panic and social anxiety, as those conditions are also initiated by conditions in your brain. For example, if you have a panic attack or experience embarrassment in a social setting, you associate the activity you were doing with the panic or social embarrassment, and then when an opportunity to do that activity comes up again, you begin to think, "What if I panic or mess up?" You begin to think about the consequences, and those thoughts lead to more anxiety.

Of course, when you have what-if thoughts that aren't connected to any real-life situation, you eventually realize they were wrong. Your husband got home (again) without having a car accident. You were able to go grocery shopping without panicking. You got through the birthday party without making any major social blunders. Realizing this, you feel somewhat better. But then, because your brain activity causes you to feel anxiety without a real-life cause, you start to feel the anxious thoughts all over again and begin another cycle of what-if thinking. Again, this kind of anxiety is "a condition looking for content."

When you can begin to see this pattern in yourself, you are on the path to recovery. Once you have noticed that your anxious thoughts did not come to pass and the anxiety was unnecessary, you can say to yourself, every time a new worry pops up, "Aha! A new anxiety! I don't have to believe this is any truer than any of my previous what-if thoughts!"

ASSESS YOURSELF

Anxious thoughts can be very convincing, even when they aren't connected to any real-life problem.

Are You Plagued by Anxious, What-If Thoughts?

Check all of the following statements that describe you.

- ☐ I am constantly wondering if I have bothered people at home or work.
- ☐ I often wonder if physical sensations I have could be signs of a disease.
- ☐ I spend time researching symptoms on the Internet to reassure myself that I'm not sick.
- ☐ I review my work and my calendar repeatedly to see whether I have forgotten or missed something important.
- ☐ I spend hours or days feeling anxious, as if something bad is about to happen. (I wait for "the other shoe to drop.")
- ☐ When someone calls me or says in person that he or she wants to talk, I immediately assume I will be chastised, fired, or told I have done something wrong.
- ☐ I have often gotten rid of one anxious thought only to have another pop up with the same intensity.

If you make a mistake, no matter how small, do any of these apply to you?

- ☐ I think over and over about what bad things can happen when I make a mistake.
- ☐ If I make a mistake at work, I spend hours worrying if I will get into serious trouble, even if I'm not sure anyone has noticed it.
- ☐ If I suspect I have made a social error, such as forgetting a name, dropping food on someone's carpet, or laughing when someone was being serious, I

---

think that friends will talk about me or stop liking me. I can feel sick for days about it.

☐ I have anxious thoughts for days or even weeks prior to an activity during which I might have a panic or social-anxiety attack.

☐ I think about mistakes I made in the past and wonder if I could still get into trouble now.

If you checked any of the boxes in these two lists, do the following thought-stopping method when you notice anxious thoughts coming on. If you checked three or more boxes, it means that anxious thoughts are interfering with your life and you might need all the various interventions that go with thought-stopping.

There are many methods you can employ to conquer anxious thinking. As you review the methods below, consider which fit your thought pattern best and start with those. As you begin to control anxious thoughts, you will eventually recognize how fear and anxiety trigger thoughts and how you can intervene on the sensations of anxiety and fear before you are caught up in yet another what-if thinking scenario.

THOUGHT-STOPPING AND THOUGHT REPLACEMENT

The basic model for ridding yourself of anxious thoughts is the thought-stopping and thought replacement method, which has many permutations and applications.

The first step is to recognize the tricks that anxiety plays on your mind. As mentioned earlier, anxious thoughts can be very convincing, but you need to learn to tell yourself, *My anxious thoughts are not true or valid.* (Again, this is for times when the anxious thoughts are not connected to a real-life problem. If your house actually *is* burning down, or your boss actually *did* put you on probation, then your anxious thoughts are perfectly reasonable. The key is recognizing the difference between something that is *actually happening now* and what anxiety is *tricking* you into believing *might* be happening or *could* happen.)

If you can't do that, you must spend time understanding why you think your anxious thought is useful and *challenge that assumption* until you are clear that the thought is worthless to you. For example, suppose you are worried that your husband is planning on leaving you—despite a lack of evidence proving he's dissatis-

---

Thought-Stopping and Thought Replacement

1. Know your anxious thoughts are not true or valid, and directly tell yourself, "This 'what if' thinking serves no purpose!" If you cannot do that, figure out why you believe your anxious thought is useful and *challenge that assumption* until you believe that the thought is worthless.
2. Whenever you notice the anxious thinking, quickly and firmly tell yourself, "Stop!"
3. Immediately change the direction of your thoughts.

Figure 8.1 Thought-Stopping and Thought Replacement

fied with the relationship—and no matter how hard you try, you can't shake these thoughts. Ask yourself, "Why do I think this anxious thought is useful?" Perhaps it's because it makes you feel like you'll be more prepared for the bad news if or when it comes. Now challenge that assumption. Will you be any less able to pack your belongings and find a new place to live if you *haven't* been worrying that he's going to leave you? Will you be any less devastated about the breakup? No! In fact, your constant worrying might even be taking a toll on him and making the situation worse. Your anxious thoughts are worthless to you.

The second step is to tell yourself firmly to "stop!" whenever you notice anxious thinking. You must interrupt the negativity as quickly as you can, and do it every time you notice a negative thought pop up.

The last step is to immediately change the direction of your thoughts. I'll discuss this step of thought replacement more thoroughly a bit later.

Why must you interrupt your negativity every single time you think the worry thought? In The *10 Best-Ever Anxiety Management Techniques* and *The Anxious Brain*, I describe this process more fully, but basically, every time you think a thought, it is easier for your brain to think that thought again. You develop strong pathways in your brain that need to be erased. Every time you stop the thought without continuing it, you weaken the trace until it is eventually erased. Erasing the trace means you will be less likely to have that anxious thought in the future.

But—and this is a *big* but—the thought will bounce right back if you have nothing to replace it with. So, you must plan ahead for good thought replacements. Following are some good ways of doing thought replacement.

- Singing (Yes! It is a great choice because your whole brain gets busy when you sing.)

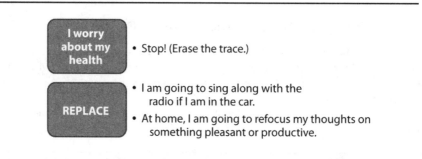

Figure 8.2 Planning Thought Replacement

- Picking a pleasant or productive thought to focus on for the day, such as remembering a fun, recent outing to the park with your grandchildren or deciding what restaurant you'd like to eat at this weekend
- Listening to music or an audiobook
- Reciting an inspirational verse or mantra
- Returning your attention mindfully back to the work you're doing when the anxious thought strikes

Why is planning thought replacement so necessary? An especially ruminative anxious thinker, Christy, remarked, "This thought replacement thing doesn't make sense to me. Why does it work? Every time I stop one negative thought, another negative thought pops up to take its place!" She had missed the part where she had to plan for a *positive* thought replacement! Figure 8.2 is an example of how this works.

MOVE YOUR BODY, MOVE YOUR MIND

A very important aspect of thought-stopping and thought replacing is helping your stuck brain move into more productive thinking. Moving your body can help enormously with this, especially if you have panic or social anxiety. "Move a muscle, move a thought" is another way to phrase this. The stuck brain literally starts to move when your muscles move, and if you couple the movement with a thought replacement technique, so much the better. Here are some ideas for moving your body:

- Listen to the audio track "Shake It Off."
- Do something around the house, especially if you've been sitting at the computer or television—put in a load of laundry, wash a dish, walk the dog, tidy up a room.
- At work, take a walk down the hall, go to the water fountain, or walk up and down steps in a stairwell for a minute while thinking about the task you will do when you get back to your workstation.
- For children, make a "kid grid" (like a tic-tac-toe chart) of nine things they can do without their parents for 15 minutes or so. Then, when they are anxious, direct them to their list of things to do instead.

FIND YOUR TYPE OF WHAT-IF THINKING

Thought-stopping and thought replacement work well with all kinds of anxious thoughts. But different types of what-if thinking present different kinds of challenges and therefore require different adaptations of the thought-stopping and thought replacement method. The following sections describe different kinds of anxious thinking and offer ways of adapting this method to each.

Rumination and What-If Thinking With a Theme

Ruminate means to think something over and over. I grew up in dairy country, and we all knew about ruminative animals such as cows. Their digestive process is to ingest, digest, and then redigest food by bringing it up to chew on for a while, then swallowing it again, then bringing it up to chew on again. Anxious thoughts can be like that. You think the same thought over and over, even though nothing about the thought changes when you do. You chew on an idea without resolving it or solving it.

Remember, anxiety is a condition looking for content. Yesterday your thoughts might have been stuck on whether something you said was misinterpreted. Today you might be stuck on whether you planned your budget the right way. Tomorrow you might fret all day about whether you took your pill and wonder if you should take one now, risking a double dose—never making an actual decision but rather fretting the day away. Ruminations can change rapidly, but the distinctive feature is that your mind is always going over and over a thought without finishing it.

Sometimes ruminative thinkers get stuck on specific topics, such as whether they have offended others, have made mistakes at work, have a disease, have hurt a pet or child in some way (often by failure to attend to a need rather than by hurting the pet or child physically and deliberately), or have failed to notice some important detail. Omission of a necessary action can be seen as being as bad as committing a wrong. People who ruminate with a theme tend to be okay when not reminded of their problem, but they also believe that if they could just resolve this one situation, they won't be anxious again. Sadly, that is rarely true. They may get a brief spell of relief, but then, because anxiety is a condition looking for content, some other what-if thought will arrive to explain the sensation of anxiety.

Help for Rumination and What-If Thinking With a Theme

If your ruminations have a theme, there is an additional and vital step to insert in the thought-stopping and thought replacement method. For some people, the theme of their ruminative thinking relates to an actual life experience. For example, if you had a parent with a chronic illness, you might be hyperalert to signs of that illness in yourself. This can make letting go of the anxious thought especially difficult. You might feel you are being disloyal to your parent, or you might believe that not worrying is tempting fate to give you the illness. When this is the case, these kinds of thoughts must be identified and resolved before thought-stopping can work.

The following diagram provides space for you to identify a rumination and plan a thought replacement to try. Remember to try it for a minimum of a week to see the change. Initially, your what- if thinking may increase a bit to challenge your resolve, but it will then drop off precipitously if you are very persistent in erasing the trace and replacing it.

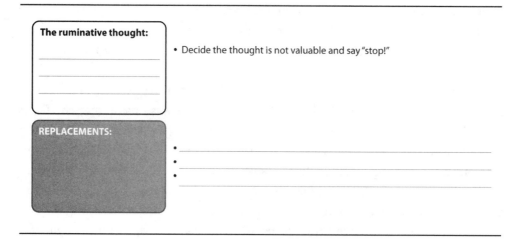

The ruminative thought:
_____
_____
_____

• Decide the thought is not valuable and say "stop!"

REPLACEMENTS:

• _____
• _____
• _____

The 10 Best-Ever Anxiety Management Techniques Workbook

Home-or-Workplace-in-Danger Thoughts

This is basically the "Did I leave something turned on?" scenario, which is a type of what-if thinking. There are many variations in addition to the "Did I turn off the coffee pot/stove/lights/curling iron?" version: "Did I lock the doors?" "Did I close the windows?" "Did I blow out the candle?" "Did I bring in the dog?" This type of thinking is often the result of inattentiveness due to the preoccupied or frantic thought process typical of a revved-up, anxious mind. These types of worriers do not stay in the here-and-now but rather rush ahead with thoughts like, "What if traffic is bad this morning?" or, "How will I get all my work done today?" or, "How did I not notice how late it is?" Distracted by these thoughts, these worriers fail to pay attention to what they are doing in the present. As they leave work or home, preoccupied with worry, they do the leaving-for-the-day tasks on automatic pilot, and once they're on the road, the what-if thinking strikes. It is accompanied by a sinking feeling in the stomach or an instantaneous flare of tingling fear. And now they are beset by two scenarios of trouble: "What if I don't go back and check?" and "What if I lose the time to go back and check?" It is a no-win situation, and they can remain preoccupied by seesawing between two bad choices.

Have you gone back to check or thought repetitively about leaving things on at home or work? Fill out the following diagram to identify your places and types of what-if thinking.

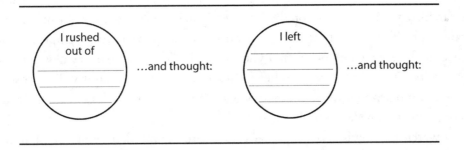

Help for Home-or-Workplace-in-Danger Thoughts

There is only one really good fix for this kind of anxiety because it is caused by inattention from being preoccupied. You must pay attention—*especially when you are already rushed and anxious.* So this is truly a simple method. Whenever you make a transition from home or from your workplace, especially when you are rushed, pay attention out loud. See Figure 8.3.

Steps to Pay Attention Out Loud

1. As you get ready to leave, take a breath and start noticing what you are doing.
2. Say to yourself out loud, "Look at this—the cord to the iron is in my hand," or "I am holding the keys I will lock the door with," or "I've got every file off of my desk that I need to take home."
3. If you are forgetful about routines you need to follow when leaving home or your workplace, make a list. It can be a one-time list, such as everything you need to do to get ready for a vacation, or a more routine list that includes everything you need to do before leaving for work or leaving for home.
4. As you are about to leave, pause. Take a deep breath. Ask yourself, "Is there anything else?"
5. Now pay attention to where you are going!

Figure 8.3 Steps to Pay Attention Out Loud

Hypochondria-like Thoughts

This is about having some kind of physical symptom and becoming afraid that it is a sign of a deadly disease. Every headache turns into a brain tumor, every sore throat is cancer, every little skin rash becomes flesh-eating bacteria. If you are beset by this kind of what-if thinking, you are wishing I would stop listing examples here—you don't need any new concerns to think about!

This kind of what-if thinking gets even more problematic when you begin researching your symptoms on the Internet. You either waste a lot of time or really scare yourself when you find all of the possibilities for what your symptoms could mean. It also gets to be a problem if you run to the doctor with every new symptom "just to be sure." You may get relief from anxiety that way, but it will be costly in time and money and it will be temporary—it won't last any longer than the next "symptom" that needs to be checked.

Watching television can further exacerbate the problem. Commercial breaks are full of advertisements for drugs that treat countless conditions you've never even heard of, and infomercials drone on about how you should better your health by taking a supplement or vitamin or by trying a new regimen of exercise with the equipment they're selling. Many news programs feature stories about diseases you might catch, your risk of exposure to contaminants, or whatever the healthy "superfood" of the moment is. Next week they will report on how all of this was wrong or harmful. Anyone who takes everything we hear in the media seriously could end up overly focused on their health, and any little sniffle or pain might seem dangerous.

Steps to Eliminate Hypochondria-like Thoughts

1. Get it out in the open. Sometimes hearing your fear aloud makes it seem ridiculous.
2. Do not go on the Internet to research. If a condition is serious at this moment, you will have indisputable indicators: significant pain or signs like high fever, out-of-control vomiting, bleeding, fainting, and so on. These are physical signs that cannot be ignored—indications that you should seek help right now. You don't need to research them.
3. For lesser symptoms that trouble you because they might be something, ask yourself, "What would be the signs that this symptom is important?" Write them down until you get the hang of this step. This would include simple awareness that the condition is worsening. For example, a rash might spread or become painful or a fever might persist. You might need to ask someone for input while you get better at this.
4. Decide when you will evaluate your symptoms again. For example, you might decide to check on your rash in 3 hours and if it is still the same, you'll check it again 24 hours later. Do not keep checking beyond that agreement with yourself on when to check.
5. Do not seek reassurance from others—rather, seek information. For example: "I am worried about whether I should take medicine for my allergies. I heard it can be hard on my heart and I don't know if that is true." Identify one knowledgeable person you could ask about that.
6. Then do the thought-stopping and thought replacement as described earlier.

Figure 8.4 Steps to Eliminate Hypochondria-like Thoughts

Help for Hypochondria-like Thoughts

The key is knowing when to take your symptoms seriously and when to recognize that your fears are exaggerated. Once you've recognized that your fears are exaggerated, you must use thought-stopping and thought replacement to eliminate them. See Figure 8.4. You may need a helper to listen to you go through these steps in the figure a time or two to be sure you are accurately answering them.

TRANSFER YOUR WORRY TO ANOTHER PERSON

While this may seem like an odd suggestion, I know almost every reader has done this without realizing it. If you ever used an accountant (or a computer program) to do your taxes, you transferred your worry to another person (or a software program) to make sure taxes were correctly filled out and that you got the most out of your deductions. Any time a person with anxiety can reasonably consult with a professional for advice, this might be wise. For example, seeking the advice of an attorney during divorce or a court appearance might go a long way toward relieving anxiety.

But I am also aware that people with anxiety may overconsult, especially in seeking medical reassurance. Or you may be a person who immediately goes to the Internet to search for reassurance regarding an anxious idea that you have. I will discuss the problem of reassurance-seeking in Chapter 9. But at times consulting experts is a very good idea. The point is not that consulting should *always* happen, but when you can't turn off worry or when you don't have the skill to handle a problem, transferring your worry to someone else is a good idea. Here are some examples:

- *Planning elder care:* There is a whole industry now for helping families find the best setting for care and the most cost-effective plan for that care. Most of us don't have the knowledge to do that on our own.
- *Post–primary care treatment for addiction recovery:* It is likely that families will not have the best ideas for how to help a person maintain a recovery program, so taking the lead from social workers, counselors, and medical staff regarding next steps can be a relief.
- *Individual education plans:* If your child needs an individual education plan (IEP), this is without a doubt a situation where you will want to utilize the knowledge of school counselors, psychologists, occupational therapists, and all the other specialists who might be called in to plan when a student is in need of academic assistance.

There are many other special circumstances where you may be worried about your own ability to handle a problem or worried about another person and how to help. The basic idea of transferring worry is that in situations where you don't have the knowledge, skill, or clarity of thought to know what to do about a situation, you will want the assistance of someone who does know. Rather than worry about it or mentally go over what you don't know how to handle, seek out the person who does know: a mentor, adviser, family friend, coach or favorite auntie, or whomever you trust and get that person's input. Then follow that person's advice! Do not rethink when you have decided to transfer your worry about whether you know enough. Consider making a S.I.M.P.L.E. plan to transfer a specific worry you have to another person.

TOO-MUCH-TO-DO RUMINATION

There are times in life when the need to accomplish tasks is truly burdensome. You might be working and also going to school, or you might be a single parent needing to work for income as well as raise children. However, people who have difficulty prioritizing work, planning, or following through (as you might if you have attention-deficit disorder) may feel overwhelmed even without an exceptional burden of extra work. Either scenario can lead to anxiety and panic.

One of my clients, Brock, felt that he had fallen apart since starting an internship at school. He was expected to quickly learn all the tasks the job entailed and deal with all the new people at the job site. At the same time, he had a pile of journals to read for his internship seminar class. He felt panicky and was plagued by "What if I fail?" thinking. To deal with his stress, he began playing video games—often for hours at a time—which did provide a distraction and give him some relief but obviously didn't solve his problem of having too much to do. Brock needed a plan to get his work done, he needed to prioritize his tasks, and he needed to get started. Only then would his anxiety diminish.

Make a Plan

The best solution to this kind of unproductive thinking is learning how to plan and prioritize. The following chapter goes into detail about planning. I only mention it here in the context of what-if thinking because it is common for people who ruminate to review a situation over and over without deciding how they will handle it. A good plan will eliminate unnecessary thinking, but there is one caveat: once you make a plan, follow it to its end point! Don't revise your plan over and over—that is just what-if anxious thinking in disguise.

Do the Worst First

This one little method can help a lot to stop your fretting. The slogan "Do the worst first" is a simple reminder to do what you do *not* want to do, but that you must do, as soon as possible. If you're going to worry all day about what you have to do (like make a phone call you don't want to make, or pay the bills), just do it first and save the worry. What a relief! There are four simple steps to follow:

1. Identify what you are putting off and notice how much you think about it.

2. Then decide when exactly you are going to do what you have been putting off.
3. Now do it!
4. Finally, notice how you feel when it's off your mind.

Fill out the following diagram to help you do the worst first.

The thing I am avoiding: _____
How much is it on my mind? _____

When will I do it? _____

Accountability: Did I do it? YES or NO

How do I feel now that it is done? _____

Make a List With Time Frames

Parents, people who work two jobs, people who work and go to school—all face a multitude of tasks that will at some point seem like too much to do. If this applies to you, consider creating a list with time frames to keep your expectations of yourself reasonable and your anxiety at bay. False expectations about how much you can do will usually make you anxious, and this kind of list is the best remedy.

Begin by making an accurate appraisal of how long (in minutes) each thing will take, and then prioritize the items according to which are most important. When you can identify how much is possible for you to get done in a day, you can have accurate expectations about your day. Prioritizing your tasks resolves the frantic feelings about what you are not getting done. The basic steps are listed in Figure 8.5.

You may be skeptical, but there is power in this kind of list: it makes you face reality. If you can't get a task done, then you can't get it done. If you have a list far longer than can be accomplished in a single day, try the following adjustments:

List With Time Frames

1. List everything you have to get done. If a task requires several days to complete (such as grading your English students' final exams) break it down into smaller units (such as reading and grading just five exams).
2. Next to each item, list how long it will take (in minutes). If it involves traveling someplace, like picking up dry cleaning, include the transportation time.
3. Then prioritize the list, numbering each task, with #1 being the highest priority.
4. Now, identify how much time you have in the day to devote to the items on your list (in minutes).
5. Finally, draw a line under the items that will use up the amount of available time you have.
6. Once you know your limit, you can relax your expectation to do more. That is all you can do for one day.

Figure 8.5 List With Time Frames

1. Remove items with later deadlines. Keep a separate list for those.
2. If, when you see what you are *not* going to do on the day's list, you react by saying, "Oh, no! I *have* to get that done by today!" (for instance, return a pile of library books due that day), then you need to change your priorities to accommodate what is most pressing. It is also possible that you will have to deal with the reality that you may miss a deadline. That may involve asking others for an adjustment or extension or telling someone you won't be able to complete an expected task. It can be a great relief to admit you are not going to get something done and set a new, more reasonable deadline.
3. Don't focus on what you can't do. Just focus on what you will get done and feel good about it.

THE S.I.M.P.L.E. PLAN TO STOP ANXIOUS THOUGHTS

You will do yourself a favor if you start working to eliminate what-if thinking right away. Pick one type of anxious thinking to start with, and make a S.I.M.P.L.E. plan that incorporates one of the methods listed in this chapter. Figure 8.6 shows a sample S.I.M.P.L.E. plan; a blank one for you to fill out follows it.

S.I.M.P.L.E. Plan to Stop Anxious Thoughts

S: What is the *symptom or situation?*   My "what if" concerns are totally preoccupying my thoughts about the new car I got. What if I paid too much? What if it has a recall? What if I find there was a much better choice for me? You name it, I am thinking about it!

I: What is the *impact on my life?*   I get another thought like this every time I get into the car, and every time people mention cars, I get a sick feeling. I can't even enjoy the new car.

M: What *method* am I trying?   I am going to do thought-stopping and thought replacement, and I am going to write a Post-It note every morning to remind myself to think about something pleasant whenever I notice I am thinking about the car.

P: Practice plan.   I will spend a minute every morning writing at least two positive things to think about. Then I will say them out loud once to myself. I will remind myself once each morning that my "what if" thinking is a waste of time.

L: Lifework.   I will post the note on my cash register at work and on the dashboard of my car so that I see it and can remind myself of my goal.

E: Evaluate.   After each week I will see if I am able to ride in my car or hear people mention cars without feeling bad.

Figure 8.6 S.I.M.P.L.E. Plan to Stop Anxious Thoughts

A FINAL WORD

Everyone has experienced what-if thinking at some point. Life sometimes throws us situations that are genuinely troubling or that are likely to result in serious trouble. But there are times when our what-if thinking gets out of hand—when it has little or nothing at all to do with reality. "What if I break my back and get paralyzed on the football field tonight?" "What if my three-year-old grows up to be a drug addict?" In reality, most what-if thinking is a waste of time and only reinforces anxiety.

S.I.M.P.L.E. Plan to Stop Anxious Thoughts

S: What is the *symptom* or *situation?* _____
_____
_____

I: What is the impact on my life? _____
_____
_____

M: What *method* am I trying? _____
_____
_____

P: *Practice* plan. _____
_____
_____

L: *Lifework.*_____
_____
_____

E: *Evaluate.* _____
_____
_____

Regardless of whether the what-if thinking is about something real or is just the result of your anxious brain, the question is *how much* your anxious thoughts take up your mental time and make you feel worse. Remember that what-if thinking is an effort to resolve anxiety (albeit an effort that doesn't work, as a new anxious thought will pop up after you've resolved the previous one). The challenge is to stop the anxious thought and replace it with a productive one that *will* eliminate anxiety. Using the methods in this technique should provide you with relief and bring you back into a life free of anxiety.

NINE

Technique #7

Contain Your Worry

Everybody worries, but people with generalized anxiety elevate worry to an art form. They take normal worries and develop them into monstrous impediments to clear thinking, enlarging them out of proportion to reality by excessive rumination. As you worry, you might even fear you are crazy because the kinds of things you're concerned about become so excessive. Your logical brain knows the things you worry about are unlikely to happen, but in your gut you feel as if they could. Containing the worry to one time or one topic may seem an impossible hurdle, but there are effective ways to do just that, with relief from anxiety being the welcome result.

The intensity of these kinds of worries is due to the highly active brain commonly seen in people with generalized anxiety. That active brain actively worries. But your active brain can help you, too—giving you the energy to remain persistent in *controlling* your worry.

Worry is insistent. It feels important. But when you persistently work against it, worry abates. That is the goal of this chapter: to get worry back down to normal proportions.

ASSESS YOURSELF

Out-of-control worry isn't just a nuisance—it can negatively affect your entire life, interfering with everyday functioning and robbing you of the pleasure you once felt in doing things you enjoy.

Do You Need to Contain Your Worry?

Check all the statements that describe you.

☐ My worry is hard to control; it creeps into my thoughts all day.

☐ I am so preoccupied with my worries that I rarely feel joy anymore.

☐ I cannot pay attention. My worry interferes with giving my attention to the details that enrich or inform my life.

Total number of boxes checked _____

☐ I spend a lot of time feeling concerned about the outcome of projects I undertake at home or work.

☐ I worry that every fever and cough my child has is going to escalate into a life-threatening illness.

☐ Whenever I hear about a potential health risk from a food (such as artery-clogging saturated fats), I immediately stop eating it and get it out of the house.

☐ I have worried about whether I've fed guests food that might cause food poisoning.

☐ I have worried that I will be put in jail for mistakes on income-tax forms or failure to comply with some detail that has legal repercussions.

☐ I've had serious concerns about becoming homeless, even though I am well educated and have a good job that I'm not currently in danger of losing.

☐ I cope quite well with real, even disastrous, problems.

Total number of boxes checked _____

If you checked one of the boxes in the first list, you will want to use the methods presented in this chapter. If you checked two or more boxes in the second list, pay *special* attention to all the methods in this chapter and seriously consider getting additional support in your effort to be persistent about containing your worry.

When a person is no longer able to shrug off worry, it is time to take charge and learn how to manage it. No one can avoid worry altogether in the course of life, but anyone can contain worry. This chapter takes into account the reality that, at times, people can't just "stop worrying about it," as their family and friends tell them to do. They instead have to employ specific methods to contain their worries.

GET THE RIGHT REASSURANCE

Do you try to calm down by getting reassurance from someone else? Do you ask people to tell you that what you worry about can't happen? You may believe you won't worry anymore if you can just get the *right* solution or the *right* information, and this leads you to ask other people for reassurance. Essentially you are asking, "Can you tell me my worries are unfounded?" You want to be reassured once and for all, but the reassurance ends up being only temporary. You may feel better for a while, but inevitably another worry crops up.

Typically, people who worry find a flaw in the reassurance: there will always be one factor you forgot to include in the discussion, and now—darn it!—the reassurance is not complete. This is why Internet searching becomes such a time-consuming pastime for worriers. You can search and search without actually bothering your family and friends for reassurance. But reassurance-seeking on the Internet is a trap that makes worry worse and doesn't teach you how *not* to worry in the future.

The *right* reassurance is reassurance that you are competent to handle problems. You don't feel better when people tell you everything will be fine without addressing the content of your worry. But you *will* get some relief from your worry if you remind yourself that even if the worst *does* happen, you will be able to deal with it.

At this point, you will need to include others in your effort to contain your worry. People you turn to for support and reassurance will need some information to help you make good progress. Getting the right reassurance requires you to give instructions to friends or family. Have them read this portion of the workbook and give them your own, personalized "wrong reassurance versus right reassurance" reminder (the blank form for this follows Figure 9.3).

The following sections describe the right reassurance and wrong reassurance for each type of anxiety.

Reassurance for Generalized Anxiety

For people with generalized anxiety, the first step in securing the right reassurance is getting the worry out in the open to see if it is connected to a real problem or is simply the result of your anxiety looking for content.

Once the problem is defined, the right reassurance consists of ascertaining that you are competent to handle the consequences of your problem: "If it turns out there is a problem, you will figure out what to do." Figure 9.1 gives examples of the right reassurance versus the wrong reassurance.

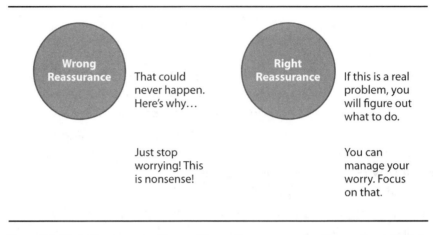

Figure 9.1 Right Reassurance Versus Wrong Reassurance for Generalized Anxiety

Reassurance for Panic

The right reassurance for panic is *not* "Oh, you won't panic." It is "Even if you do panic, once it's over, you can go on with what you were doing." Or, "Even if you panic, you will get through it." Or, "If you do panic, even if it's a lot of panic, you have all the skills you need to cope with it." Of course, you *do* need the skills to stop panic, so if this reassurance is to be successful, make sure you've worked on Chapters 4 ("Breathe") and 7 ("Stop Catastrophizing").

The first step for getting the right reassurance for panic is to acknowledge that your fears are (1) that the panic will be *horrible*, and (2) that the outcome—dying, going crazy, or losing control—will be *awful*. In fact, neither catastrophe is true.

It may be true that if you panic, you will feel embarrassed or will want to escape, so remind yourself that you have the skills to cope with it.

Finally, remind yourself that you are competent to handle your panic and the consequences of panic. Figure 9.2 gives examples of the right reassurance versus the wrong reassurance for panic.

Reassurance for Social Anxiety

Because people with social anxiety are especially sensitive to feelings of anxiety, they are more inclined to fear feeling anxious. They particularly fear other people noticing they are nervous. If you have social anxiety symptoms, you will need the social skills to accomplish your goals as well as the practice to make them work well. Pay special attention to Chapters 10 through 12 to develop and practice a plan.

The 10 Best-Ever Anxiety Management Techniques Workbook

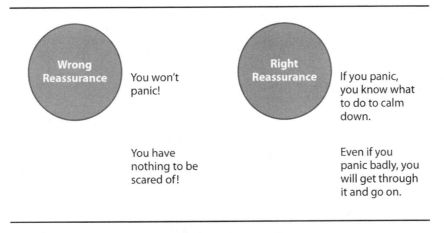

Figure 9.2 Right Reassurance Versus Wrong Reassurance for Panic

At the beginning, the right reassurance for people with social anxiety is, "You are working on your goals, and I can help you with that." Once you have worked on your plan and practiced it, your right reassurance might be, "Even if you show some anxiety, you know how to get through it. And remember, people are more accepting than you may think."

In general, the right reassurance for social anxiety includes (1) openly acknowledging what *exactly* you think will happen, and (2) reminding yourself that you have the competence to handle both your fear and the consequences of feeling afraid ("You can tolerate feeling afraid, and you can handle it if you look nervous"). Figure 9.3 gives examples of the right reassurance versus the wrong reassurance for social anxiety.

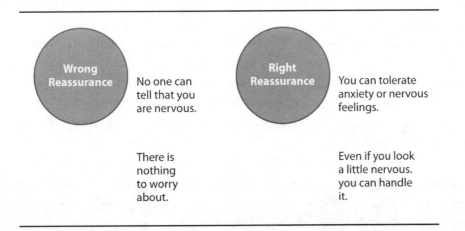

Figure 9.3 Right Reassurance Versus Wrong Reassurance for Social Anxiety

Write in your own reassurance phrases on the following diagram.

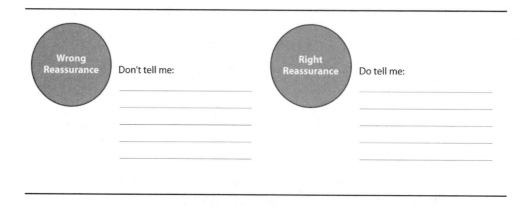

MAKE A PLAN

People with anxiety are often extremely competent in handling real problems. Real problems have real solutions; with an unambiguous problem and an unambiguous solution, anxiety disappears. (Remember, anxiety is a response to ambiguity.) A clear plan of action is a godsend to an anxious mind. That's why planning is a terrific anti-worry measure.

Consider your typical type of worry: "What if my car breaks down on vacation?" "What if I fail the test?" "What if no one asks me to the prom?" "What if I don't get this job I applied for?" All of these situations have a common element—if they *do* happen, a response will be in order, and in each case, a plan could be made. But worriers sometimes get confused between what might require action and what is just a worry. If you can't identify a specific problem that can be solved, then you're probably just having an anxious thought, and thought-stopping and thought replacement (see Technique #6) are in order. For example, ruminatively thinking, "What if I lose my job?" may be a pointless (though disturbing) worry if you have a secure job in a stable company. But if you are worrying about a *real* situation—"My company is going to lay off 30% of the workforce when this location closes, and one of those people could be me"—then you have an actual possible problem that can be addressed by coming up with a plan.

Even when there *is* a real situation that can be addressed by a plan, however, some people simply worry about the situation without moving to the next step of identifying the actual problem. Mandy was a good example of that. She called in distress, saying, "I lost my job!" and asked for an emergency appointment. When she came in, I asked her what she wanted to discuss. She was taken aback. "I lost my job!" she exclaimed, wondering if I'd heard her the first time. "Yes," I replied, "but how is that a problem?" With a look of puzzlement on her face, she said carefully, "*I . . . lost . . . my . . . job.*"

"Indeed. And how does losing your job cause a problem in your life?"

Then it dawned on her: "Oh. Because I lost my job, now I have the problem of needing another source of income."

As a reader, you may be thinking, "Well, that's obvious! Losing your job is the same as the problem of needing a new source of income." But don't be quick to leap to such conclusions. Instead, consider Stephanie, who also lost her job. Stephanie had worked at a nonprofit organization that supported the arts. Married to a successful lawyer, she didn't need to work for financial reasons—she worked because it provided her with a sense of purpose in life and because the job gave her status in the community. Both Mandy and Stephanie had lost their jobs, but their *problems* were very different, as were the solutions. To solve *her* problem, Mandy needed to find a new source of income. Stephanie, on the other hand, needed to find a new way to give her life purpose, possibly by doing volunteer work or taking up a new activity. By getting stuck on the *situation*—"I lost my job"—you can feel desperately worried but unable to resolve your anxiety because you haven't defined the problem.

Once you've identified the problem, you can begin figuring out a plan to address it, which will be a big relief to your anxious mind. The final step of the process is evaluating your progress. The following sections describe the whole process in detail.

Identify the Problem

What is the problem? Get very specific—for example: "I want a shot at a scholarship and I have three Bs. I want to raise them to As." Or, "I want to go to the winter dance with a date and I have not yet been asked." Write your problem in the following diagram.

My problem is:	_____
	_____
	_____
	_____

Now, what is the goal? Goals direct solutions. For example, suppose your problem is that you haven't been asked to the winter dance. There could be several different goals associated with this problem. One might be, "I want to go to the dance with John Doe." A very different goal might be, "I don't want to sit at home feeling lonely while my friends are at the dance." Each of these goals would lead to different solutions. In the first case, you might not want to accept any invitation to the dance unless it's from John Doe. In the second, you probably *would* accept any invitation to the dance—or just decide to go without a date. Write your goal in the following diagram.

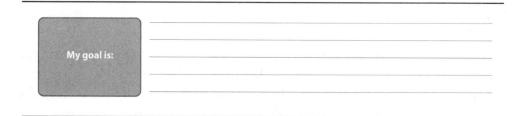

Brainstorm Solutions

What are possible solutions to achieve your goal? List every option. Anxiety narrows your thinking because it puts blinders on your attention and creativity. Sometimes listing wrong choices makes it easier to see the right one. A lot of anxiety is generated by feeling you have no choice or control in a situation. But you always have a choice, even if the choice is to continue on the path you are already on.

Another trick your mind might play on you is, "What if I didn't think of *everything*?" To circumvent this, ask yourself, before you wrap up action steps, "Is there anything else I have to consider or do?" If you answer, "No, this should cover it all," then your worry "What if I didn't think of everything?" is just a trick your anxious brain is playing on you. Say to yourself, "I will not replan my plan. I will evaluate my progress on _____ ." Then do thought replacement.

Write down all the possible solutions to your problem in the following diagram.

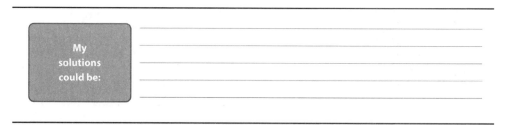

The 10 Best-Ever Anxiety Management Techniques Workbook

Select One Option

Now pick one "best" solution and identify the action steps you'll need to follow to do it. Remember, you are picking the best solution—not the perfect solution! People often get stuck worrying, "What if I choose wrong?" But the truth is that there are many good solutions; there is no perfect solution. Say to yourself instead, "I can change my mind later if my evaluation shows this solution is ineffective." This is the purpose of evaluation!

Write down your solution and the action steps it requires in the following diagram.

Solution:	_____
Action Step #1	_____
Action Step #2	_____
Action Step #3	_____
Action Step #4	_____

Tell Yourself, "Stop! I Have a Plan!"

Expert worriers may find themselves worrying even *after* they have a plan. This is where thought-stopping comes in. If you feel those what-if thoughts popping back up, tell yourself, "Stop!" and then add, "I have a plan!" Then use your planned-ahead thought replacement.

Evaluate How the Plan Is Working

It is necessary to plan evaluation points. If you don't, you will just continue to worry: "Is this the right step? Is this working? What if it doesn't work?" Remember, you are evaluating your *progress*—not whether the problem has been completely resolved. Depending on your goal, achieving the solution may take some time. But working *toward* that goal is something you can begin immediately, noting whether you've been successful in achieving each of the action steps on the path toward solving the problem. Decide which action steps need evaluation and when.

Here's how to do it:

1. Decide what the first reasonable point to evaluate your progress is, and mark it down on your calendar. For example, if your goal is to find a new job, a reasonable first evaluation point might be in two weeks ("Have I sent out my résumé to at least five different companies? Have I received any requests for interviews?"). If your goal is to mend a friendship with someone you had a falling out with, your first evaluation point might be quite a bit later. *Don't monitor daily unless it is called for*—that's just another way of letting what-if thinking creep in. If you notice yourself doing this, say, "Stop! I will think about this on _____ ," and then do thought replacement.

2. If obstacles come up, you can revise your action steps.

3. Evaluate the results on the day you marked down in your calendar.
   a. If you were successful, note what you did to make it work.
   b. If you were unsuccessful, either revise your action steps or consider trying a different solution.

4. After evaluating your results, set a new evaluation date and mark it on your calendar. Continue with this process until the problem is solved.

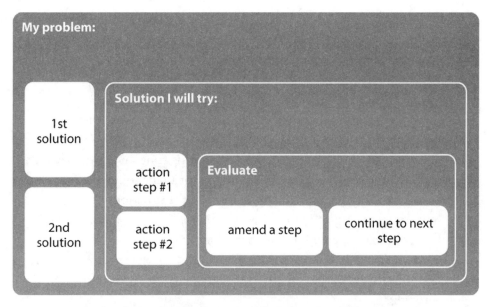

Figure 9.4 The Process of Making a Good Plan

An Additional Note About Evaluating

In Chapter 10 on changing self-talk, I will discuss how anxiety causes you to look for what is wrong more than what is right. When evaluating your progress toward your goal, look at what is working! What is going right? How did you make that happen? What do you want to adjust to make it better? Stay far away from what is wrong or not perfect.

Figure 9.4 shows a short form of the entire planning process.

WORRY WELL AND ONLY ONCE

People with anxiety disorders worry when worry is unnecessary, worry when there is no value in worrying, and, mostly, worry to the extent that it ruins their lives. "Worry well and only once" is a method that takes worry seriously *one time only* and sorts out what is a real problem from what is unrealistic worry. It involves examining what you can control versus what you can't, what you can do something about versus what you can do nothing about. And it helps you make arrangements for when it would be a good idea to worry again.

When people face troubling circumstances, they worry. Most anyone would. This method turns worrying into a combination of planning and thought-stopping for situations that are serious and have a measure of ambiguity, such as when you are undergoing medical treatment, experiencing legal trouble, or waiting to hear whether you passed the state bar exam.

Here is the process:

1. Start by listing all the things you could be worried about. Dissect your problem.
2. Then, do anything that must be done at this time and do not delay. Make phone calls, talk to someone, write or make something, repair, clean, or take any action that will improve the situation.
3. Sometimes taking action is necessary only *if the problem should occur*. In that case, make a plan for "What if it happens?"
4. Ask yourself, "Is there anything else I need to worry about?" Your brain needs to hear a "no." If you say yes, you need to redo steps 1 through 3.
5. Set a time when it will be necessary to think about the worry again, and write it down somewhere: "If x happens, then I will do y. But if x doesn't happen, the next time I will review this worry is on March 15." (Note this on your calendar: "Worry about x.")
6. Whenever the worry pops up again, declare, "Stop! I already worried!" and use thought replacement techniques from Chapter 8.

Let's look at an example of how this works. Cornell had high blood pressure. He was worried about the side effects of medication, and he also worried about the possibility of a stroke or other medical complications. Figure 9.5 shows how he set up "worry well and only once."

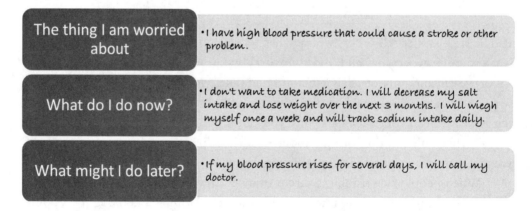

The thing I am worried about	• I have high blood pressure that could cause a stroke or other problem.
What do I do now?	• I don't want to take medication. I will decrease my salt intake and lose weight over the next 3 months. I will wiegh myself once a week and will track sodium intake daily.
What might I do later?	• If my blood pressure rises for several days, I will call my doctor.

The 10 Best-Ever Anxiety Management Techniques Workbook

Is there anything else I need to worry about?	• I guess not.
When should I worry next?	• I won't worry about this for 90 days. It is in my calendar, so I won't forget to worry then. I will monitor my blood pressure and if it is high or rises, I will talk to my physician about medication.
What will I do if worry pops up?	• Whenever I find myself worrying about my blood pressure, I will say, "Stop!" and I will remind myself the day to worry is marked in my calendar. Then I will think about something pleasant.

Figure 9.5 Worry Well and Only Once

Now make your own "worry well and only once" plan by filling out the following diagram.

All the things I'm worried about:	•———————————————— •———————————————— •———————————————— •———————————————— •———————————————— •————————————————
What do I need to do right now?	•———————————————— •———————————————— •———————————————— •————————————————
What might happen later that I must respond to, and what will I do then?	•———————————————— •———————————————— •———————————————— •————————————————
Is there anything else I need to worry about?	YES (repeat steps 1–3) NO (go to next step)

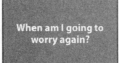

When am I going to worry again?	Date and time: _____
When the worry pops up, say: "Stop! I already worried!" Then do thought replacement.	My thought replacements: _____

DITCH YOUR DREAD

The sensation of dread can *precede* the thought that there is something to feel dreadful about. Sometimes this is referred to as "free-floating" anxiety, but it can be recognized by the pit-of-the-stomach unease that all people associate with dread. The circle of dread is shown in Figure 9.6.

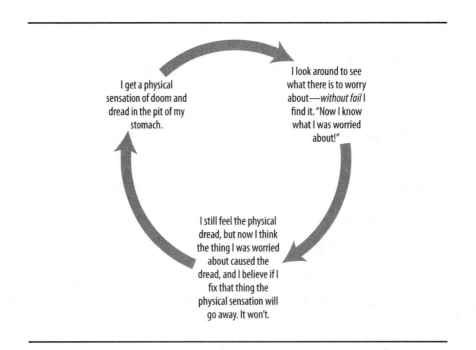

I get a physical sensation of doom and dread in the pit of my stomach.

I look around to see what there is to worry about—*without fail* I find it. "Now I know what I was worried about!"

I still feel the physical dread, but now I think the thing I was worried about caused the dread, and I believe if I fix that thing the physical sensation will go away. It won't.

Figure 9.6 The Circle of Dread

The 10 Best-Ever Anxiety Management Techniques Workbook

If you feel dread, this method is going to be of considerable use to you. But be forewarned: it requires a leap of faith—*you must believe that dread can precede worry and be present for no good reason.* Although worry can indeed make you full of dread, for many with generalized anxiety, it is dread that creates the worry. The sensation of doom is an outcome of the neurobiology of anxiety. But it's simple to get rid of.

1. The first step for people who have dread is to come to believe that they won't fail to notice a real problem. Do you have the ability to recognize a problem?
2. Next, notice the dread. Don't ask what the reason for the dread is; rather, ask, "Is this sensation dread?"
3. Then, find a way to relieve the sensation:
   - *Through diaphragmatic breathing.* With just a minute to breathe and engage in muscle relaxation, the body can relax and begin to let go of the dread at the physical level. (See Chapters 4 and 6 for these techniques.)
   - *Through thought-stopping and thought replacement.* Say to yourself, "Stop! I will not fail to notice a real problem." Then immediately use a thought replacement.

The following statements will help you ditch your dread. On an index card, write down the one that most appeals to you and then carry the card with you.

- "A feeling is just a feeling."
- "Dread does not need a reason. I will not go on scan mode to find one."
- "Breathe, distract."
- "I will not fail to notice a real problem. I don't have to look for one."

CLEAR YOUR MIND

Do you feel your mind jumping around or find it hard to stop it from running down a track? Do you need to:

- Get everything off your mind to focus on something important, like studying for a test or writing a report for work?

- Clear away tangled thoughts to think clearly about something?
- Empty your mind to rest?
- Leave work behind to enjoy time off or come into the house ready to be home?

If this is what you need, "clear your mind" is the method for you. There is more than one version, but all of them are simple.

The "Container" Version

This version of the method is included on the audio download "Contain Your Worry." Basically, it goes like this:

1. Imagine a container sitting in front of you. It is a container that can hold all of your concerns. The container is open and ready to receive whatever you want to put into it.
2. Now, think about (but don't mull over) all the things that are pressing on your awareness or asking for your attention. Anything—good or bad, big or small—can go into the container. Give each thing a name.
3. When everything has been named and put in the container, place the lid on the container and set the container aside.
4. If the next thing you want to do is sleep, invite a peaceful thought into your mind.
5. If you want to focus on something, invite into your mind thoughts about the thing that you want to be thinking about.

Other Versions

Some people are not fond of the container imagery, and if that is the case for you, or if you just want more than one way to clear your mind, here are other ways to use this method:

- *The list*. Write down your thoughts in the form of a list. Be very brief. Use one or two words to list the things that occupy your thoughts. Then put the list in a drawer, briefcase, or other place where it will literally be out of sight (and out of mind.)
- *The God box*. This version comes from Al-Anon. The "God box" is

used to hold slips of paper, each of which has a thought that is to be turned over to God.

- *Pictures in a backpack.* This version works best with children. They can write or draw a picture of their thoughts or worries and put it into a worry box, a worry file, or worry backpack that a counselor or teacher keeps for them. With that adult, they can periodically open the backpack and see what's in it. They will learn that worry passes, and that if bad things happened, they lived through them and coped.

- *Worry dolls.* There are small dolls in a box or bag from Guatemala that can be purchased from global marketers or import stores. The legend is that a person can hand the concerns or worries of life over to the dolls and the dolls will take the worries away. The lid is literally put on the box so that the dolls can carry the worry away and ready themselves for the next batch of worries.

CONTAIN YOUR WORRY IN TIME

There are situations that you will worry about when you probably should worry. No, really. There are things not under your control, things you can't plan for and that are so important it would be impossible *not* to worry. What are these? What if someone you love is in danger? Perhaps she is in the military, a firefighter on duty, doing a stint in Doctors Without Borders, or another kind of worker in a war zone or health-risk area. What if you are letting an adult child go live outside your home after having that child with you recovering from drug addiction? *You are going to worry* about relapse or safety. What if someone you love is suffering from cancer or has a life-altering disease? *You must feel worried* about their survival and well-being! Other situations may fit this issue too.

My client Craig was worried about his mother, who had just been diagnosed with cancer that was very far advanced and from which she was not going to recover. He found it hard to concentrate at work because he felt so worried about her. He used this method to contain his worry. Figure 9.7 demonstrates how he did this.

Craig decided to worry every day before he left for work. Since his mother loved the out of doors, he wanted to sit where he could see greenery, and he put a favorite picture of her on a table near the chair to focus his attention only on her. For many people, this is an opportunity to pray for the well-being of the one they are worried about, and I encourage people to use the time for that, incorporating

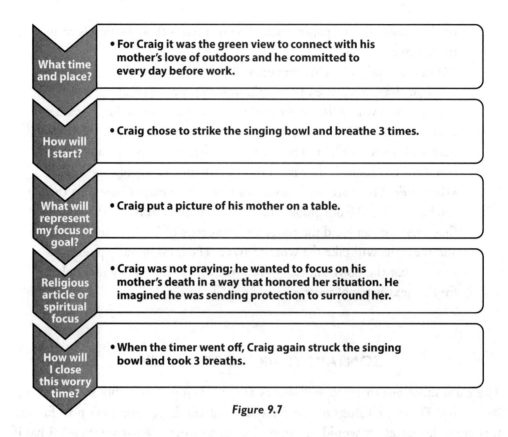

What time and place?
- For Craig it was the green view to connect with his mother's love of outdoors and he committed to every day before work.

How will I start?
- Craig chose to strike the singing bowl and breathe 3 times.

What will represent my focus or goal?
- Craig put a picture of his mother on a table.

Religious article or spiritual focus
- Craig was not praying; he wanted to focus on his mother's death in a way that honored her situation. He imagined he was sending protection to surround her.

How will I close this worry time?
- When the timer went off, Craig again struck the singing bowl and took 3 breaths.

Figure 9.7

standard prayers and using articles of faith such as rosaries, crosses, prayer shawls, incense, or whatever is religiously meaningful. Craig was not a person who prayed, but he had practiced some meditation, so he decided he would start his worrying by striking a singing bowl and taking three deep breaths. He also needed to think about how to worry, and he decided that he wanted to transform his worry in some way to make it more positive. He wanted to think about his mother and to honor what she was going through, yet not think about it all day long. He decided to imagine worry as a protective force, sent to surround his mother with protection from fear while she faced the end of her life. He set a timer for 10 minutes, and when it went off (clearly signaling the time to quit), he would strike the singing bowl one more time and breathe. This example is unique to Craig but demonstrates one way to do this.

But what should *you* do? Worry! And here is *how* to worry. I just gave an example of how Craig used this version of containing worry. When you make a *ritual* of worry, you spend 10 minutes a day on your worry. The rest of the day, when the troubling situation comes to mind, you tell yourself, "Yes! And I will worry again tomorrow!"

Rituals have the same components for everyone:

1. *Regularity of time and place.* Set a timer, especially at first. Your brain is already in the habit of interpreting the ding of a timer to mean that you're done.
2. *Starting with a specific signal.* For example, you could say the same words or a prayer, light a candle, or bow your head or body. Craig chose the singing bowl.
3. *An object that represents the person or the situation.* Craig chose a picture, but you could use any object.
4. *Religious articles that are meaningful* to enhance your prayer.
5. *The same closing.* When the timer goes off, snuff out the candle, say a closing prayer, or strike the singing bowl as Craig did.

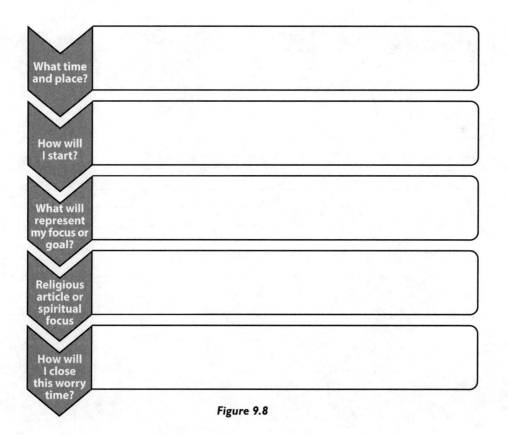

Figure 9.8

Figure 9.8 is a worksheet for containing your worry in time. Remember that this method should always adapted to your own individual spiritual stance.

Craig and others who have used this method have found that they have almost immediately been able to contain their worry within the worry time and then focus on other parts of their lives, such as the work they have in front of them. As this method becomes a habit (you do it until the situation is resolved), you may end up using it for any worry that is important and persistent.

S.I.M.P.L.E. Plan to Contain Worry

S: What is the *symptom* or *situation*? _____
_____
_____

I: What is the impact on my life? _____
_____
_____

M: What *method* am I trying? _____
_____
_____

P: *Practice* plan. _____
_____
_____

L: *Lifework.* _____
_____
_____

E: *Evaluate.* _____
_____
_____

The 10 Best-Ever Anxiety Management Techniques Workbook

THE S.I.M.P.L.E. PLAN TO CONTAIN WORRY

This chapter has presented several ideas for containing your worry. Some will seem more like what you need than others. Pick one idea that seems best for you and work out a S.I.M.P.L.E. plan to begin using it.

A FINAL WORD

These ways to contain your worry all have an ultimate goal of "turning it off"—of giving your worried mind a chance to rest and to calm down that "hot" worry activity in your brain. If you are persistent and consistent in using these methods, your brain will calm down and generate less worry. Control of your anxious mind is won slowly, purposefully, and persistently. If you are willing to put in the effort, the payoff will be a calmer, quieter, less anxiety-generating brain.

PART IV

Managing Anxious Behavior

TEN

Technique
#8 Control TMA (Too Much Activity)

Are you a high-drive kind of person? Do you describe yourself as a Type A personality? Do you prefer moving to sitting? Do you prefer hiking to lying in a hammock? There is nothing wrong with being active in this way, but unless you take care of yourself, you may become a person with too much activity—a TMA. A high-drive personality is usually evident in childhood, and although being energetic is certainly not a problem in itself, a high-drive style can easily turn into generalized anxiety as people get older and busier. See Figure 10.1 to note how this develops.

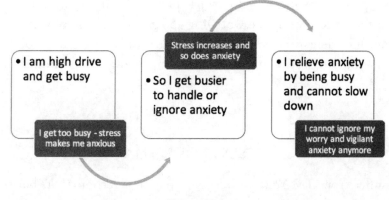

Figure 10.1

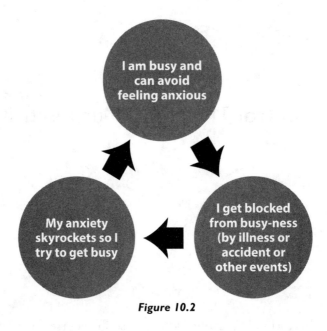

Figure 10.2

When you have anxiety, too much activity (TMA) serves a purpose. High activity *diminishes* anxiety in the person whose brain is set up with this energy. But high-drive people present an anxiety dilemma: they also get anxious when they're *not* actively doing something, either mentally or physically, and that becomes a problem if they are blocked from busyness, as you can see in Figure 10.2.

If you have TMA, you probably feel agitated when you hold still, especially when you haven't planned how to use your downtime, and your feelings of anxiety may escalate rapidly. Your response to this may then be to get very busy and try to ignore the sense of anxiety.

You are probably wondering, "What in the world could be wrong with being a high-drive, productive person?" You don't want to give up your level of productivity; you just want to give up the worrying and general feeling of anxiety that permeates your life. Here is the good news: As you assess yourself and look at methods to diminish your anxiety, your energy will be put to good use in mastering your anxiety.

ASSESS YOUR TMA

Do you suffer from TMA? If you do, you may not recognize it, but the people around you certainly do! Do people often say to you, "I don't know how you get so much done!" or "Where do you get the energy to do that?" or "Don't you ever sleep?" or "How can you take this on when you have so much else to do?" If you hear those kinds of questions, read on.

TMA and Students

I see many young people in high school and college who already qualify for the TMA label. These are students building impressive résumés for college and winning numerous awards for athletics, arts, or academic achievements. Their parents may be too pleased with their success to realize there is a problem brewing.

If you are in high school or college and are feeling anxious, see if TMA is making your anxiety worse.

CONTROL TMA

One of the highest-drive people I ever met was a woman I admire very much for her successes. She was also, sadly, one of the most miserably anxious people I've treated in my practice. Darla was a CPA running her own business. She also managed to be at every activity her children participated in, spearheaded the local high school fundraisers, and was active in a major community volunteer organization. She was felled by anxiety when she broke her ankle and no longer had the mobility to maintain her active lifestyle. She was supposed to take six weeks off—by week three she was so consumed by worry that she could no longer sleep. Her previous level of activity had discharged her anxiety, and being forced to remain still and stop her work seriously intensified her anxiety.

This holds true for many people with TMA. They will benefit on many levels by addressing this brain-based energy and the anxiety that often accompanies it. They can start by relaxing their typically tense bodies. The track on the audio download, "Tense and Release Progressive Muscle Relaxation," is a terrific way to change the "uptight" bodies that come with TMA.

Plan for Dreaded, Unexpected "Free" Time

This is a brief strategy but genuinely helpful to the overly driven TMA person. Life always produces unexpected times when you must hold still in one way or another. Appointments get canceled, people don't show up, airline flights are delayed, social events are postponed. If you have TMA, you probably find it especially challenging to hold still unexpectedly. It's as if you get "brain freeze" about what to do next. You feel that you have to choose the most important, useful thing—even if it's just a way to relax or do something nice for yourself. For example, if your son calls to say he's staying at the neighbor's for dinner, you spend the whole time he's gone deciding if it would be better to get a manicure or take a bath. Worried about not making the best choice, you get anxious (and probably get neither the manicure nor the bath in time).

Even a snow day for the TMA student can produce a brain freeze about what to do. A particularly talented senior in high school told me she "lost an entire weekend" when a drama activity was canceled due to inclement weather. She slept late, watched movies, and drank coffee with friends. Toward the end of the weekend, she became upset when she realized she could have been scrapbooking the pictures from the last show she was in—something she'd told herself would be a good idea if she ever had time. She moaned, "Now I don't know when I will ever have time again to get that done!"

The "if I ever have the time" list is a great way to relieve this anxiety. Whenever you say, "If I ever have the time, I want to _____ ," add that activity to the list, and keep the list handy. The activities you list can include anything at all—calling a friend, building shelves in the garage, baking bread, taking a bath. *Anything* can go on this list. Try it now. Look around your home or office and see if you can find five things you will do if you ever have the time.

1. _____
2. _____
3. _____
4. _____
5. _____

Now:

1. For each item, note how long it will take.
2. Carry the list with you on paper or in your mobile device, and whenever you're faced with unexpected "free" time, select an activity from the list that fits the available time. (Because you're already certain that you want to do it, you will be able to select something quickly, and your anxiety about choosing will be relieved.)
3. As you complete tasks, cross them off, and keep adding new "if I ever

The 10 Best-Ever Anxiety Management Techniques Workbook

have time" items when you think of them. This is *very* satisfying for people with TMA.

Your list might look something like that pictured in Figure 10.3, If I Ever Have the Time.

If I Ever Have the Time . . .

1. ~~I will organize those pictures into a book on Shutterfly (2 hours)~~

2. I will finally put that diploma into a frame (15 minutes—or 45 if I have to buy the frame)

3. I want to go to that new shop with art supplies and see what it has (30–60 minutes)

4. I will go through my files and throw away notes and papers I do not need (60 minutes)

5. I will put shelves up in the garage and stack things on them (6 hours)

Figure 10.3 If I Ever Have the Time . . .

Identify and Counter Perfectionism

When people who are anxious seem like perfectionists, they often don't see themselves as such. They don't feel wedded to making everything perfect, as if order and correctness were goals in themselves. Rather, perfectionism for them is a way to ward off anxiety, even if they don't realize it. The underlying belief is, "If I do enough, carefully enough, then I will never make mistakes and I won't have to worry." And this works well—until the person makes a mistake. Then he or she has to raise the bar on being better, more careful, and more thorough. And this, of course, reinforces the perfectionism.

You may not realize your anxiety will come back no matter how hard you work. You already know that people want you to work hard—after all, you get results! But you may fear that if you ever let down your perfectionist guard, things will *completely* fall apart and be *absolutely, terribly* wrong and others will blame you *entirely.* (Note the extreme language here—"completely," "entirely." It's the way the thought process goes.) In other words, you believe that *everyone* sees your mistakes as intolerable and as proof of your unworthiness. The person with TMA perfectionism often sees no way out.

Identify Perfectionism

To get a better sense of how perfectionism plays a role in your personal life, write down answers to the following questions.

1. I have a strong sense of *personal* responsibility for the outcome of work, social, or family activities, especially when other people could be reasonably expected to do some of the work. How do I show that?

   _____

   _____

   _____

   _____

   _____

2. I hear myself using extreme words like "always," "never," and "this is terrible," and I see the consequences of mistakes as being extreme (failure, ruin, etc.). Here are some examples:

   _____

   _____

   _____

   _____

   _____

3. I am very watchful about details, and I think it's a good idea. Here are the ways I am detailed-oriented:

   _____

   _____

   _____

   _____

4. I can't always see the difference between "good enough" and "perfect" when it comes to my responsibilities. Here is an example:

   _____

   _____

_____

_____

_____

See the Price of Your Perfectionism

Do any of the following apply to you?

- Have you been blamed (unfairly) for being controlling and not been seen as helpful or careful?
- Have you taken on extra work that no one asked you to do and later felt overworked?
- Do you firmly believe you would have fun if you could only find the time?
- When you are responsible for an activity (such as hosting a party), do you feel a lack of pleasure and fun despite the fact that the activity *should* be fun?
- Do you feel completely exhausted and have no idea how or when you will recover?
- Are you noticing that you feel anxious, even when paying very close attention to details, in one arena of responsibility?

If you answered "yes" to even one of the above, it means your perfectionism is having negative consequences on your life. It's time to work less and figure out another way to let go of anxiety. Pick one of the following and commit to a specific way to try it in the coming week:

- Commit to letting others do a part of what you feel responsible for, *even if you believe they won't do it as well.* Let someone else bring dessert, clean the bathroom, write up the meeting notes, or make the Power-Point slides.
- Every time you catch yourself using "all" or "never" language, tell yourself to stop it immediately. Doing this will undermine the idea that perfection is possible. A slogan for anxious perfectionists should be, "Perfection is impossible." Follow that slogan with, "If something is impossible, then I have no obligation to try for it."
- Plan for nonperfection. Actually planning a nonperfect performance of some responsibilities will work better than noticing accidental

imperfection. So, go ahead and buy cookies instead of making them, show up five minutes late, don't print off the agenda for a meeting, or forget the ketchup for the picnic. Obviously don't pick an imperfect performance that could get you in trouble, but see if others can tolerate you as an imperfect being. This won't be quite so anxiety-provoking as an unintentional mistake because you will be doing it on purpose, and you can perhaps begin tolerating the anxiety of being less vigilant against any errors.

Instructions for the perfectionist include:

- Let someone else step up to the plate (e.g., don't agree to mow the lawn just because your kid complains when you ask her to do it, don't agree to babysit at the last minute, don't write that report your colleague is dragging his feet on, don't agree to cover someone else's shift). You may well find that when you hold back, someone else will step up. Even if the work doesn't get done, it's not end the world.
- Observe and evaluate how people respond to the imperfect work of others.
- Don't do work others are responsible for. Observe how this affects the attitudes of others and your own anxiety level.
- Finally, plan to not finish some work that you would otherwise have knocked yourself out to do. Miss a deadline by a little bit, or just don't do something. You may have to get advice on what you can let go, but do it. (Pick something that seems minor in the eyes of others. Here are examples: Don't go out to buy the right napkins for the party—use paper towels. Ask if you can have a one-day extension on a project— see what the boss or teacher says. Don't prepare the agenda in writing before the staff meeting. These kinds of details that you believe are major are probably going to turn out to be inconsequential most of the time.)

Now commit to doing it:

I will _____

_____

_____

On this date or in this situation _____

_____

_____

Finally, evaluate the outcome:

Did anyone ca re whether I was perfect? Their names are _____

_____

_____

If something went wrong unexpectedly, how did I and others cope?

_____

_____

Can I tell the difference between the consequential things and inconsequential things? What did I note? _____

_____

_____

This evaluation will help you make future decisions about what you can drop and what is essential.

Identify Perfectionistic Procrastination

An irony of perfectionists who procrastinate is that they often do so as a way to set boundaries on the amount of time they spend at a task, whether it is party preparation, schoolwork, or big reports for work. Rosario was a college sophomore who reversed day and night and was very stressed out. She indicated that her coursework included writing a lot of short papers and said, "I can get a three- to five-page paper done in five or six hours, so I start at midnight and email it or take it to class the morning it's due." She said if she started at noon (a reasonable idea for six hours of work), she would revise the paper all night anyway, so she just started at midnight to control the amount of time she put in.

But another type of perfectionistic procrastinator is the one who won't start a project until he knows he can do it perfectly, reading manuals and preparing while week after month after year goes by in preparation but not completion of the job. Or perhaps the task is one you know you can do but don't have the time to do completely and correctly all at once, so you put it off until the day there's time to do it right. This can be in any realm, from planting flowers around the back porch to buying a couch to organizing a desk, a workshop, or a file of vacation photos.

Another type of perfectionistic procrastinator just won't try something new because he doesn't know how to do it—avoiding the reality that all of us make mistakes when we learn. This person just can't tolerate the anxiety, so he won't try the new activity or task.

Ask yourself:

1. Do I often get work done as the deadline hits because I was researching or preparing or very busy with something else that was also important? What are some examples of that?

   _____

   _____

2. I describe myself as a person who works better under pressure, and I often wait until there is a deadline that forces me to get work done. It looks like I procrastinate, but, really, I am so busy. I am always doing something even if I am not working on the things that are most essential. I try to get in every important task, and there are just so many. But I won't allow myself to miss deadlines, so I always get it done. What are some examples of that in my life?

   _____

   _____

3. I don't like to start until I know I can do it perfectly, so I often research or prepare until the last minute. What are some examples of that in my life?

   _____

   _____

4. I am always waiting to tidy up and get organized until I have enough time to do it the right way. My work space (or my closets, or my desks or my files) are a mess and it makes me incredibly anxious. But I will do it as soon as there is time to do it right. What are some examples of that in my life?

   _____

   _____

If these examples resonate with you, consider whether you are willing to set some boundaries on the time you spend. I suspect you will need some help to decide how much time is reasonable and which things can be done less than perfectly and still be acceptable so that you can research or prepare less. As you prepare a S.I.M.P.L.E. plan, think about who you know and trust to give you sound advice about how much time to spend, what tasks to let go, and whether you know enough to begin a task. As a TMA perfectionist, you may be locked into your way of doing things and may well have to borrow someone else's brain for a bit until you learn to tolerate the anxiety of not being perfect.

ACHIEVE THE RIGHT BALANCE

Achieving balance in life results in emotional, physical, and mental well-being. People with TMA get out of balance unintentionally. There are times, of course, when it's important to devote more attention to one part of your life. For example, if you're preparing to sell your company, getting your agency ready for inspection, or studying for a final exam, it might be perfectly reasonable to work 12 hours a day for a circumscribed period of time. But shifting back to balanced activity is often a problem for the TMA person, who can easily continue on that work, work, work trajectory even when other aspects of life are also important. How often have you heard someone say, "I know I should exercise and take care of my health, but . . . ," or, "I know I *should* spend more time with my kids, but . . . ," or, "I know it would be *better* if I took time for myself every day, but . . ."? These kinds of statements indicate a lack of balance.

Keep Track of Your Time

People with TMA can be very, very good at thinking they are sufficiently balanced, even when others in their lives don't see it that way. They need objective evidence. If you're one of those people, here's a way to get that evidence.

1. Keep track of what you're doing with your time for at least a week every day. (If the week is not representative of your normal routine, do it for two weeks.)
2. Divide your week into hours with 15-minute time slots in each day. Fill it in as you go—not at the end of the week—to keep from fooling yourself. See Figure 10.4. (Note that there are 16 hours in the example here, assuming you spend 8 hours sleeping. If that is not the case, add the extra waking hours and record what you do with them.)

	M	T	W	Th	F	S	S
Hour 1	15 m. bkfst 45 m. shwr						
Hour 2	45 m. commute 15 m. email						
Hour 3	15 m. email 45 m. mtgs						
Hour 4	60 m. mtgs						
Hour 5	30 m. return calls 15 m. talk w/ colleague 15 m. snack						
Hour 6							
Hour 7							
Hour 8							
Hour 9							
Hour 10							
Hour 11							
Hour 12							
Hour 13							
Hour 14							
Hour 15							
Hour 16							

Figure 10.4 Keep Track of Your Time

The 10 Best-Ever Anxiety Management Techniques Workbook

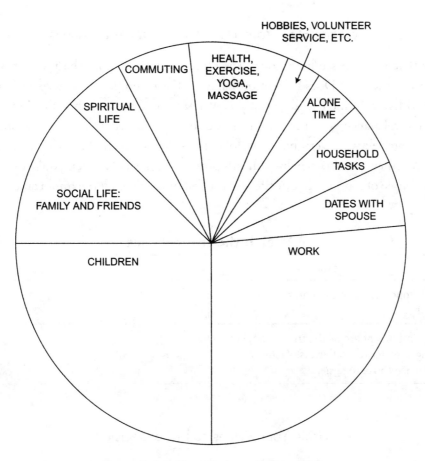

Figure 10.5 Is There Balance in Your Life?

3. Now make a list of categories into which your daily activities fit. Include *everything*—personal hygiene, watching television, eating, time with friends, work, and so on. (If you are having trouble getting all your work done in a reasonable amount of time, divide work activities into separate categories in your list—email, phone calls, meetings, paperwork, etc.)

4. Add up the minutes you spent on the activities in each category.

5. Use these totals to create a pie chart showing the amount of time you spend on each category. See Figure 10.5 for an example.

Evaluate How Your Use of Time Fits Your Values

Now that you can see how you're spending your time, does the proportion of it make sense to you? Does it seem off balance? For example, are you spending more time with family and friends when you want to spend more with your spouse? If so, begin to rebalance your life with this one method: increase the time you spend on something you want very much to do and less time on something that matters less.

Another exercise to help with this process—especially when you're evaluating just a couple of aspects of your life—is the following "weigh the importance" chart.

Weigh the Importance

Question	Answer
How important is it that I do this task/activity?	
How important are all the things I am *not* doing in order to do this task/activity? What are those things?	

Using Your Values to Make Decisions

If you're having a hard time making a decision in any situation in which you have to make a choice (e.g., whether to take a job, buy a house, go to one school versus another), it's probably because you're not taking your values into consideration. Try the following exercise.

Using My Values to Make a Decision

Identify a situation (e.g., taking a new job, buying a house, going to school).

_____

Make a list of every important aspect of the situation that affects your decision.

_____

_____

_____

_____

_____

_____

_____

_____

Now sort the list according to a hierarchy of what is the most significant. Sometimes it's easy to see what is important, but sometimes it's not so clear. You can clarify your values by comparing one significant item to each of the others on your list. What's the new hierarchy, starting with the most important thing at the top?

1. _____
2. _____
3. _____
4. _____
5. _____
6. _____
7. _____
8. _____

REDIRECT TMA TO HAVE SOME FUN

If you have TMA, you are probably overworked and underrelaxed. One client of mine, Betty, described it well. She said she liked to entertain. It was fun for her to plan, cook, and create a party. She also said she didn't remember much about her parties because she was so busy being a nonstop perfect hostess—the "fun" was hearing that her guests enjoyed themselves. This is classic TMA—too much work blotted out the fun.

Laughter Is a Good Start

Laughing is a great way to increase good feelings while discharging physical energy. Recreating fun and getting the relief of laughing is serious therapy for the serious person. Ask yourself, "What makes me laugh?"

Look for "Busy Fun" Opportunities

Because people with TMA don't like to sit still, they often find "busy fun" activities (such as a day of gardening, a 40-mile bike ride, or hitting every garage sale in town on a Saturday morning) more relaxing than activities that are more leisurely (such as a massage or soak in the tub). When choosing busy fun activities, make sure you distinguish between those that are pleasurable to *do* and those that are pleasurable because they give you a sense of *accomplishment* afterward. The goal is to find activities that you enjoy as you actually do them. Ask yourself these questions:

- Was the activity itself pleasurable or unpleasurable?
- When I recall each aspect of the activity, are most of them pleasing?

TMA AT DIFFERENT AGES AND IN SPECIAL CIRCUMSTANCES

Although TMA is more prevalent in adults in their working years, it can affect people of any age. Following are some guidelines for spotting TMA in children, adolescents, and the elderly. (See the Resources section for more information on getting help for these age groups.)

A warning sign for anxiety in children is being serious, tense, and constantly busy. Observe:

- Have parents set up too much activity because of their own anxiety about failing to push a child to explore his or her potential in every way possible?
- Is all of the child's play time organized?
- Is something in the home—such as abuse or a family secret—keeping the child vigilant?
- Are there possible mental health issues, such as obsessive-compulsive disorder?
- Is the child's anxiety specifically related to his or her social skills?

Adolescents who are constantly tense may have anxiety that drives them to perfectionism, but they may have real problems in school or extracurricular activities that they need help with. Assess for such problems by asking:

- Are the adolescent's peers very hard on him or her? Is the adolescent being teased, bullied, or embarrassed?
- Are there classroom demands for public performance?

- Do teachers, coaches, or other authority figures have expectations the adolescent fears he or she cannot meet?
- Is all of the adolescent's leisure time organized?

In these cases, anxiety management must include specific problem-solving for peer problems and extracurricular or classroom demands. You will be able to see whether the adolescent can relax after the environmental problem has been solved. If the anxiety persists, anxiety disorder treatments will be necessary.

Elderly adults usually have the fewest demands for performance, but as people with TMA age, they may face problems managing anxiety when their activity is limited by health and mobility. Loss of activity can increase anxiety. Also be sure to check on:

- Health changes (e.g., a problem with vision or hearing that could be an obstacle to social engagement)
- Losses of friends
- Changes in residence

Devise a plan to reestablish activities that compensate for the changes.

A FINAL WORD

People with TMA will always want to be active. The key to diminishing the negative effects of TMA is keeping balance in your life. You can discharge tension through positive activity and let go of the perfectionist behavior that keeps anxiety high. Your energy is going to help with this because you tend to do what you decide to do. Here's hoping you decide in the direction of balance and fun!

THE S.I.M.P.L.E. PLAN TO CONTROL TMA

If you have TMA, chances are good that you will want to do everything at once. Remember that there is no perfection, only progress! So select one of the methods outlined in this chapter and make a S.I.M.P.L.E. plan to start on it. For example, let's say you pick "life balance." Your S.I.M.P.L.E. plan might look something like Figure 10.6.

S.I.M.P.L.E. Plan to Control TMA Life Balance

S: What is the *symptom or situation?* *I am spending 12 hours a day on my commute and workday.*

I: What is the *impact on my life?* *I am not exercising at all and I am more sluggish and gaining some weight.*

M: What *method* am I trying? *I will increase the amount of time I spend walking each day by going out at lunch for a 30-minute walk. On weekends I will do at least one very brisk walk for 45 minutes.*

P: Practice plan. *I don't need to practice walking, but I will put gym shoes and socks in the backpack I take into work with me so I have the shoes there.*

L: Lifework. *Barring emergencies, I will walk every day during my lunch break after I've had something to eat.*

E: Evaluate. *I am going to tally my time walking on a card, and I will keep the card on the refrigerator so I can see the balance shift toward better self-care.*

Figure 10.6

Now fill out your own S.I.M.P.L.E. plan.

S.I.M.P.L.E. Plan to Control TMA

Method: _____

S: What is the *symptom* or *situation*? _____
_____
_____

I: What is the impact on my life? _____
_____
_____

M: What *method* am I trying? _____
_____
_____

P: *Practice* plan. _____
_____
_____

L: *Lifework.* _____
_____
_____

E: *Evaluate.* _____
_____
_____

ELEVEN

Technique #9
Talk Yourself Into Changing Your Behavior

Are you afraid of being afraid? When you suffer from panic or social anxiety disorder, fear of fear causes you to change your behavior. If you've had a panic attack while in a crowded supermarket, for example, you probably now fear going to the supermarket at busy times. If you've found yourself stammering at company meetings, you probably now fear speaking up at future company meetings. This fear of feeling afraid leads you to avoid those situations. Unfortunately, this kind of avoidance also begins to curtail your freedom in increasingly severe ways. And it keeps you from developing skills to deal with discomfort and to try doing things in a different way.

Fear affects you based on the way you think about it. If you say to yourself that you can't stand being afraid, you will avoid situations in which you may feel fear. If you say to yourself you will get through it even if you feel afraid, you will be less inclined to avoid situations in which you might want to participate. You can see how that is working in your life by looking at your self-talk—the running dialogue you have with yourself in your head. By changing your self-talk, you can begin changing your avoidance behavior. This technique reflects how changing the mind and changing behavior are intimately linked.

Let's start by looking at avoidance behavior—the biggest challenge for people with anxiety, especially panic and social anxiety.

ASSESS YOUR AVOIDANCE

Avoidance of certain places and situations may begin at a fairly low level—for example, if you had a panic attack during a theater performance, you may avoid going to future theater performances, which may not be a terribly big sacrifice in the broad scheme of things. But avoidance behaviors tend to escalate, and soon you're avoiding not only theater performances but also cinema complexes, sports stadiums, and even the school auditorium where your daughter is having her first piano recital.

Are Avoidance Behaviors Beginning to Impinge on Your Life?

Check the following questions that you can answer yes to:

☐ Do you stay away from places where you might have a panic attack?
☐ When you go into a new setting, do you check how you can escape?
☐ Do you avoid television shows or news reports about topics that raise your anxiety?
☐ Do you avoid thinking about topics that make you feel anxious?
☐ Do you make an effort to avoid being observed or being the center of attention?
☐ Do you worry ahead of time about what a new situation will be like and sometimes go to check it out ahead of time to reduce your anxiety?

If you checked yes for even one of these questions, you will want to specifically identify your arenas of avoiding. Make a list of situations, places, or interactions with others that you have avoided. Here are some examples of common things people avoid:

- Going into large lecture classes at college
- Traveling by air
- Driving on a limited-access highway
- Going to the grocery store during the day
- Speaking in class or at a meeting
- Meeting new people (at work, at a meeting, at a party)

The 10 Best-Ever Anxiety Management Techniques Workbook

ASSESS THE INTENSITY OF YOUR FEAR

Now that you have your list of situations, places, or interactions with others that you have avoided, you're going to chart the level of fear each of those situations produces on a scale from 1 to 10, with 1 being low and 10 being high. Figure 11.1 illustrates how to do this. The left-hand column rates the level of fear you experienced during the times you have actually been in that situation. The middle column rates the level of fear you experience when you anticipate being in that situation again. The right-hand column rates your level of fear after you've avoided the situation.

In the example shown in Figure 11.1, the situation was "driving over a bridge." The actual times the person had driven over a bridge produced a high level of fear, so she colored in the boxes through the number 10. The morning she had to drive to a location that required crossing a bridge, her fear was at a very high 9. When she

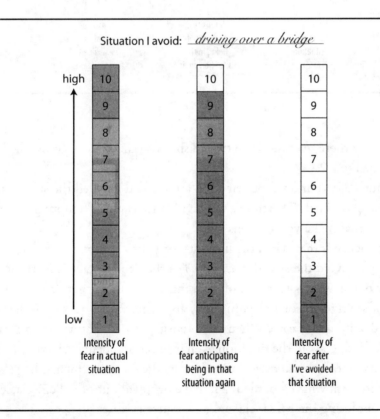

Figure 11.1 Assess Your Intensity of Fear

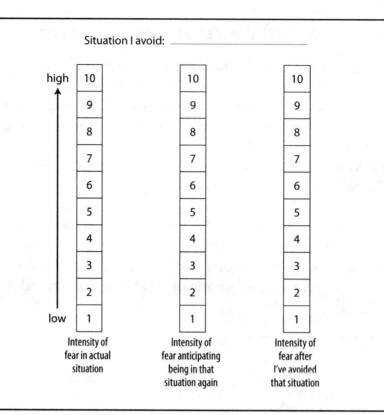

Situation I avoid: _____

high	10		10		10
	9		9		9
	8		8		8
	7		7		7
	6		6		6
	5		5		5
	4		4		4
	3		3		3
	2		2		2
low	1		1		1

Intensity of fear in actual situation

Intensity of fear anticipating being in that situation again

Intensity of fear after I've avoided that situation

decided, halfway there, to cancel the trip so she wouldn't have to cross the bridge, her fear dropped to a 2.

How much did your level of fear drop after you'd avoided the situation? You probably felt a lot of relief! This shows why avoidance is such a tempting way to deal with situations that make you anxious.

My experience is that when the intensity of your anticipatory fear is between 5 and 7, you will avoid the situation *except when* the need to face it is stronger. For example, a woman who is terrified of walking into an emergency room because she's afraid of seeing someone bleeding may force herself to go despite her fear if her child needs emergency care. When the intensity of anticipatory fear goes to 8 or above, people tend to avoid the situation even if the consequences are very negative. I've had clients who have canceled important medical appointments, have walked off airplanes after they have boarded, and have dropped out of college classes even though it meant losing their financial aid and course credit.

The 10 Best-Ever Anxiety Management Techniques Workbook

If you want to learn how to stop avoiding, the first step will be *decreasing* fear and *increasing* motivation. The way to do this is by changing your self-talk and learning to tolerate your feelings without fear of them. The track on the audio download, "Managing Uncomfortable Sensations," is a place to start that process. Once you've decreased your fear and increased your motivation, you can begin learning the skills you need—skills to reduce anxiety and skills to do the activities that frighten you.

ASSESS YOUR SELF-TALK

Again, self-talk is the running dialogue you have with yourself in your head. It's when you argue both sides of a problem with yourself, and it includes hearing in your mind the voice of a parent, coach, or acquaintance.

All too often the self-talk we engage in expresses criticism and doubt. "Should I try to talk to that attractive woman at the end of the bar? I guess not—I'm sure she wouldn't be interested in me, and I'd probably say something dumb." "Should I accept my friend's invitation to go to the baseball game? The last time I was in a stadium, I panicked, and I'll probably panic again. I guess I should tell him I can't go."

Is Your Self-Talk a Problem?

Check the following questions that you can answer yes to:

☐ I tell myself that I will make a fool of myself if I try something new.
☐ I tell myself that people won't like me.
☐ I tell myself that no one else answers questions incorrectly or stumbles when trying to explain things in meetings or classrooms.
☐ I tell myself that I won't be able to stand it if I blush or get embarrassed and others notice it.
☐ I tell myself people won't notice if I don't show up or participate, so it's okay if I don't go to the event.
☐ I tell myself that I will feel scared, and I can't stand feeling scared.

If you checked yes to two or more of these questions, you need to learn how to begin changing your negative self-talk.

Negative inner dialogue increases fear and anxiety and causes us to anticipate failure and rejection, thus preventing us from taking action that would be positive for us. The biggest problem with self-talk, especially when we don't realize we're doing it, is that it has the ring of truth. *You tend to believe what you say to yourself.*

And self-talk is predictive. If you tell yourself that something is going to be scary, chances are excellent that you will perceive it as scary. Then the emotional part of your brain will think, "This is scary!" and reinforce your negative self-talk as *true*. Your brain will then go on to warn you that every similar situation will be scary, and thus a self-fulfilling prophecy about social fear or panic is born.

On the positive side, however, if you deliberately make *positive* self-statements, you may well start to believe them! That is the goal of this technique.

IS AVOIDANCE INTERFERING WITH YOUR GOALS?

Changing behavior starts with the conviction that behavior change is necessary. Is your avoidance behavior getting in the way of your goals? What do you want? To be able to go on a job interview? To be able to participate in class? To speak up at a meeting or point out your successes as your peers do? Knowing what you have to gain by facing fear or anxiety is the first step to sticking with a plan for change. And writing it down reinforces that knowledge. So take a moment here to write down your goals. What will you do if you have less anxiety? What quality of life are you seeking? What changes in relationships will occur if you feel better? Figure 11.2 is an example.

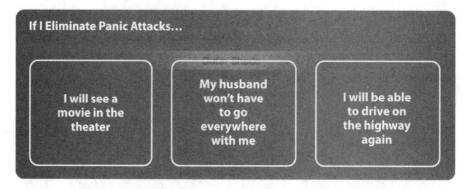

Figure 11.2 What Will I Get When I Get Rid Of Anxiety?

The 10 Best-Ever Anxiety Management Techniques Workbook

Now fill in your own.

Goal: _____

Outcome: _____	Outcome: _____	Outcome: _____
_____	_____	_____
_____	_____	_____
_____	_____	_____
_____	_____	_____

When you can see what your goals are, it is time to look at what is stopping you. How is your self-talk interfering with getting rid of anxiety? If you have anxiety, you have developed some beliefs about your condition. You may believe it is impossible to control, or you may believe that panicking means you are going crazy. Those beliefs get in your way.

GET EDUCATED: THE PRECURSOR TO CHANGE

It's important to remember that anxiety is a protective response. Your brain and body try to protect you by warning you of possible risks. For example, if you're hiking on a mountain trail and suddenly come face-to-face with a bear, you're probably going to feel very anxious. Your heart rate will jump, and your brain will tell you, "Run! You're not capable of fighting off this bear!" That response works to keep you safe much of the time.

The problem is when your brain and body send out "Danger! Warning!" signs when the situation isn't actually risky. Your brain might warn you, for instance, to stay away from a dinner party you've been invited to because you might embarrass yourself. Or that you're not competent to handle the anxiety you might feel being in a crowded theater. Or that your daughter has been in a terrible car accident when she's a few minutes late getting home from school. You have to learn to talk back to that warning. Changing your self-talk will help you:

- Learn to tolerate uncomfortable sensations as merely uncomfortable, not awful

- Take control of negative self-talk and eliminate it
- Act in direct opposition to false beliefs you hold about your competence
- Develop confidence that you can control fear and stop avoiding life

BASIC IDEAS TO MASTER

Before you begin looking at ways to change your negative self-talk, learn and remember the following basic ideas about anxiety and how to manage it:

- Panic, worry, and social fears can be changed by changing thoughts and behaviors.
- Social anxiety is not specifically fear of danger, but rather fear of exposure (i.e., the fear that others will observe you looking embarrassed). Blushing, sweating, and shaking are autonomic responses to being exposed. The more you tell yourself you will be humiliated, the greater the risk of these symptoms.
- Changing self-talk and beliefs is a key component of changing behavior. Beliefs drive action.
- Practicing new behavior is the ultimate way to get rid of fear.

FIND AND CHANGE YOUR SELF-TALK

The impact of beliefs about yourself, the world, and other people can be easily seen in choices you make and are revealed in your self-talk. Every small thought that creates anxiety must be identified and corrected. What are some ways to find out what you are saying to yourself?

Ask Yourself, "So What?"

People can be unaware of how they talk to themselves in self-sabotaging ways. To hear your own voice, start out by being a detective in your own life. As you go through experiences, try to objectively notice exactly what happens and what you are saying to yourself. Write down everything so you don't overlook any important details. Copy down the following questions on an index card (or put them in your smartphone) and carry it with you at all times:

1. Notice: Where am I and what am I doing?
2. Notice: What are my anxiety symptoms and how bad are they?
3. Ask yourself: "*So what* if I have these symptoms?"

Your answer to this last question will reveal your negative inner dialogue or self-talk. Take a look at Figure 11.3.

Where am I and what am I doing?
- I am in a meeting.
- My turn to speak is coming soon.
- People are looking at me.

What are my symptoms and how bad are they?
- My heart is racing, my face is probably red, and my hands are shaking visibly.
- They are pretty bad: about a 7 out of 10.

So what if I look nervous and they notice?
- I will look stupid.
- I will feel humiliated and I hate that feeling.

Figure 11.3 Finding Your Self-Talk

Now identify a specific situation you find yourself in and fill out the blank form.

Where am I and what am I doing?
- _____
- _____
- _____

What are my symptoms and how bad are they?
- _____
- _____
- _____

So what if I have these symptoms?
- _____
- _____
- _____

Counter Negative Self-Talk

Once you know what you're telling yourself, you have to replace it. There are a couple of good methods of doing this, one of which is countering negative statements by replacing them with opposites. In this method you will identify each part of an activity or situation that you want to do and then construct a list of negative thoughts you have about that specific goal. The next step is to create replacement thoughts. Then, every time you engage in the negative self-talk, you will read or say the replacement thought *immediately*. This will allow you to deliberately override your negativity and lay the groundwork for willingness to change behavior.

Figure 11.4 shows how this worked for Guy, a 22-year-old who wanted to go back to college after he had dropped out due to anxiety. He knew he had the intelligence to go to school, and it bothered him that he was working in a gas station when he could be in school. He listed his goals and then noted the negative self-talk that was interfering with doing what he wanted to do. Finally, he planned replacement thoughts and wrote them into the third column of this chart.

This was Guy's list of goals:

- I want to start school in six weeks.
- I want to talk to the admissions office about getting all my other credits accepted.
- I want to be able to talk to other students about the classes.
- I want to attend every class and not leave at any time due to nervousness.
- I want to finish school completely in two and a half years.

Now create your own three-column table, with goals on the left, negative thoughts in the middle, and replacement thoughts on the right.

Goals, Actions, Intentions	First Thought (negative self-talk)	Opposite of First Thought (positive replacement thought)
Start school in 6 weeks	I may not be able to meet that timeline. I always miss deadlines.	I have filled out applications before and I know I have time to do this. I will use my support system to encourage me.
Talk to admissions about getting credits accepted	I don't know where to go and I don't know whom to talk to there. It might not even be worth it—I bet they won't transfer credits from the junior college.	I can call ahead to get the information about whom to see and where to go. Other students figure it out, so I can too. I can't know what they will accept if I don't ask. It is worth it financially to make this effort, even if I don't like it.
Talk to other students	I will make a fool of myself. I am no good at talking to strangers.	Everyone in the class will be strangers to each other. Talking about class does not require me to be witty or tell jokes—just to talk, which I can do.
Attend every class and not leave because I am nervous	I have always run out of class.	Even if I am nervous, I can stay. I have practiced skills to stay.
Finish school completely in 2 1/2 years	I will never finish school. I don't think I have ever stayed long enough to get enough credits.	Things are different today. I have a goal, and I can stay in school even if it is hard.

Figure 11.4 Planning Replacement Thoughts for Negative Self-Talk

Goals, Actions, Intentions	First Thought (negative self-talk)	Opposite of First Thought (positive replacement thought)

Recite Affirmations

It is no surprise that self-talk contributes to failure to do and be what we want. People often fail because they believe they will fail. If you have anxiety, you fail in advance by avoiding anything that seems too tough. When we say to ourselves that we will be too frightened or embarrassed if we try, we set ourselves up for failure. Our chances of success are much better if we imagine ourselves succeeding, see ourselves doing something right. By affirming what we want to be true (about our lives, our situations, our character, our attitudes, and so on), we create the conditions for that truth.

Affirmations are a way to form thoughts that counteract negative self-talk. An affirmation is a positive statement about yourself, said aloud it as if it is already true. The idea behind affirmations is that you will more readily create the conditions for what you desire if you think and speak it aloud. For example, if you want to become more comfortable talking at meetings, an affirmation you might say would be, "I am confident and competent when I express myself at staff meetings." You say the affirmation as if the attitude and action were true right now.

For affirmations to be helpful, they must be believable and possible. Telling yourself, "I am fully capable of jumping off the high dive" when you don't even know how to swim certainly won't do you any good! First you need to learn to swim—or gain skills in public speaking if that's your fear, or learn the new computer software at work if you're anxious about your job performance. Again, affirmations are useful in combating negative self-talk only when they are believable and possible.

What reality do you want to create? Do you want to fly in an airplane? Do you want to be comfortable dating? Do you want to audition for the band or go on a job interview? Figure out what you want, and then form the right phrase. Try writing an affirmation for yourself about something you want. Figure 11.5 shows an example.

My Affirmation

What I want: I want to complete this workbook and feel less anxious when I am meeting new people.

I affirm: I am competent to meet and greet new people and confident that I can do it without fear.

Figure 11.5 My Affirmation

CHANGE THE FILTERS ON EXPERIENCE

You know that your past performance is the best predictor of your future performance. That fact might cause distress if you believe you can't change your panic or social anxieties. So you will want to develop new expectations about the future. In Chapter 12, you will look carefully at how to prepare and practice new actions so you feel comfortable doing them. But first, you must change your thinking about your ability to change behavior. To believe you really can accomplish behavior change, you must change your "filters" on your experiences.

The fact is, *you have probably succeeded far more often than you have failed*. But if you are like many people with panic or social anxiety, you tend to see only the times when you fled a room feeling like you were going to suffocate, or remember only the times when you became embarrassed. You obsess about wrong answers you gave at school, the bad throws in the game, or the times you froze and didn't speak when you should have. If you have generalized anxiety, you may remember only the times when your dread *did* precede something bad happening—even though 99 times out of 100 nothing terrible came to pass and your dread was just a false alarm.

To establish the conditions that will allow you to conduct yourself successfully, you will first need to know how you block yourself by your self-talk. Then, in Chapter 12, you will see how to plan memory-changing activities that help you live a more fulfilling and less avoiding life. You will see how you can achieve enough calmness, competence, and confidence to take action successfully.

What Do You Expect?

When you've had a negative experience, you start to filter new experiences through a lens of expecting the same bad outcome. You go on the lookout for bad experiences and don't notice positive ones. Worse, you make inaccurate generalizations about your experiences: "I panicked the last time I drove on the highway, so I will obviously panic *whenever* I drive on the highway." People with social fear *expect* to be humiliated or *expect* themselves to be unassertive, ignored, or flustered. They stop seeing the moments when other people responded warmly to them or when they succeeded socially. And people with generalized anxiety *fail to notice* all the times their dread proved to be a false alarm. The problem is that negative expectations are self-reinforcing—your negative expectations don't get challenged so continue to feel true. All of this seems to prove the self-talk true.

In these cases, self-talk—what you expect—is not accurate. It reflects specific kinds of cognitive errors that are common to anxiety, and these mental errors go unchallenged because you begin avoiding new situations that could contradict them. Figure 11.6 illustrates common cognitive errors along with examples of each.

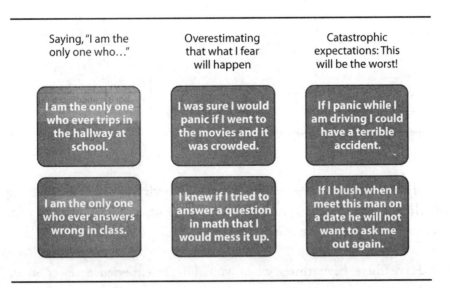

Figure 11.6 Cognitive Errors You May Recognize

Some additional cognitive errors you may recognize include:

- Underestimating your capacity to tolerate negative experience. You may believe you can't handle anxious feelings or believe you can't tolerate having something go wrong. (In fact, however, you wouldn't be doing this workbook if you hadn't tolerated plenty of negative experiences already!)
- Believing you don't have control over how you feel.
- Believing you don't have control over any part of the outcome of situations; believing you will inevitably feel rejected or embarrassed if others notice you.

Now fill in the following diagram with your own examples of these cognitive errors. You can add any other types of cognitive errors you may make, too.

Saying, "I am the only one who…"	Overestimating that what I fear will happen	Catastrophic expectations: This will be the worst!

Correcting cognitive errors starts with a search for situations that disprove these beliefs. Look at the diagram you just filled out, and list times the situations didn't have the outcome you feared.

- Have there been times when you did *not* experience rejection or humiliation? (An important note here: Even though you might have felt embarrassed, did others *actually* humiliate you? Saying that the other person probably was *thinking* negative thoughts doesn't count!)
- Have there been times when you did *not* panic in a crowded room, on an airplane, while driving, etc.?
- Have there been times when nothing bad ended up happening even though you were feeling a sense of dread?

Write down as many of these positive situations as you can—actually writing them down by hand will help you remember them. Figure 11.7 is an example of how to notice and write down a change in your filter. A blank diagram for you to fill out follows it.

Now keep up this search for positives as a regular part of countering your negative self-talk. Unlearning a lifetime of negative filtering takes some time!

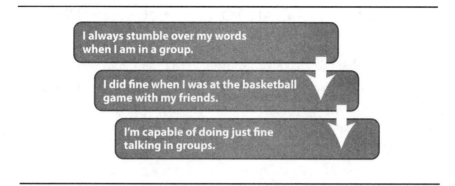

Figure 11.7 Changing Your Filter

What I expect: _____
_____

What I observe: _____
_____

My new expectation: _____
_____

A FINAL WORD

Many skills must be learned and interwoven for the best success in recovering from any anxiety problem. Changing your inner dialogue takes time. People who have not exercised for years cannot get up and run a marathon tomorrow. No one would expect them to. They would need to start with a short walk, practice it, repeat it, and extend it to be longer and faster before they could ever expect to make a long run. Every small step of progress is necessary. This is true of changing anxious behavior by changing your self-talk, too. Starting with the change of self-talk is like taking walks before getting to the run that prepares you for the marathon.

THE S.I.M.P.L.E. PLAN TO TALK YOURSELF INTO CHANGING YOUR BEHAVIOR

It's very important that you make a commitment to listening to yourself and changing the way you talk to yourself. Was there anything in this chapter that spoke to you about the way you speak to yourself? Identify a place to start, and make a plan to carry out the change. Remember that consistently changing your inner dialogue will change your behavior automatically.

S.I.M.P.L.E. Plan to Talk Yourself Into Changing Behavior

S: What is the *symptom* or *situation*? _____
_____
_____

I: What is the impact on my life? _____
_____
_____

M: What *method* am I trying? _____
_____
_____

P: *Practice* plan. _____
_____
_____

L: *Lifework.* _____
_____
_____

E: *Evaluate.* _____
_____
_____

TWELVE

Technique #10

Implement a Plan and Practice the Three Cs

This technique is about mastering the three Cs of behavior change and memory reconsolidation: calm, competence, and confidence. In this chapter, I focus on how you may acquire competence and confidence—the two steps that follow staying calm to achieve success in social engagement. And, in the process of mastering this technique, you will achieve memory reconsolidation—the literal changing of a negative memory at the level of how it is stored in the brain by weaving it together with new, positive experiences. This will do wonders to decrease your fear and increase your motivation to achieve future success.

If you practiced the techniques for breathing and relaxation, you should know about staying calm. This technique is about acquiring competence and confidence. The only way to achieve these is through life experience that expands or strengthens your knowledge and skills. If you have been avoiding situations so you don't panic or fear humiliation, then you will need to learn how to have new experiences in ways that strengthen your willingness to continue developing.

This chapter is intended to help people with panic and social anxiety (Chapter 10 was for people with generalized anxiety). It will show you how to develop competence and confidence in managing anxiety in work and social settings. Mastering this technique will require you to have worked on other techniques first so you can now devise a plan and carry it out effectively. A big part of your confidence comes from knowing that even if you still get anxious from time to time, you will be able to manage it.

EDUCATE YOURSELF ON
HOW THE BRAIN LEARNS AND UNLEARNS FEAR

You know, from experience, that your anxiety lessens when you avoid what you're afraid of. But your avoidance actually gives power to the situation you are avoiding. You may be thinking, *If I feel such relief by avoiding this situation, then it* must *be a dangerous situation, right?* Not right! In all probability there was no objective risk, but *your fear* was what made it seem dangerous.

There is just one basic principle you need to remember: you learned to be afraid by feeling afraid in a situation regardless of its actual risk. Your brain wants to make sure you stay out of scary situations—it wants to keep you safe. But the emotional part of your brain can't tell the difference between your fear of a genuine danger and the fear you generate because you *perceive* a situation as threatening. Thus, you can become afraid of being at a party, or in an elevator, or outside in a hurricane. Only one of those things is genuinely dangerous. But your brain will warn you away from all three if you have felt afraid in those situations.

MEMORY RECONSOLIDATION

Exciting research over the last few years has clarified how to make negative experiences far less controlled and directing of our lives. When you understand how this works, you will see how to set up new experiences so that you have the best chance of really changing your fear and avoidance. If you have had a bad experience, you will probably anticipate that similar experiences will also be bad. For example, if you were teased and felt humiliated because you gave a bad speech in front of a group, you may never want to do that again. Thereafter, you may avoid speaking in front of a group, and even if you pull it off by accident, you may still try to avoid it, remembering that bad outcome of humiliation. This happens to many people with performance anxiety or social anxiety.

But what if you want to change the memory of the experience itself so that it no longer troubles you? Research has made it clear that you can do that. You can plan exposures—that is, entering into experiences you would rather avoid—so that the outcome is different.

1. Activate the negative memory. You need 10 minutes and up to six hours of remembering and feeling the feelings of the bad experience if you are going to change it.

The 10 Best-Ever Anxiety Management Techniques Workbook

2. Go into the experience having prepared to succeed.
3. Carry it out successfully—have a good outcome this time.
4. Notice and validate it by rehearsing it in your mind and discussing how well it went.

These four steps—not easy to do, but well worth planning and doing—will result in a memory change called "reconsolidation" that will allow you to remember the first, negative experience differently. It is now woven together, at the cellular level of memory, with the second, positive experience. To make this work, you must succeed at what you try.

DEVELOP COMPETENCE

If you want to unlearn fear, you have to be in the frightening situation without feeling afraid. *You have to be there without the scare!* Just as you can legitimately *learn* fear by being caught in a hurricane, you can also legitimately *unlearn* fear by successfully exposing yourself to the nondangerous situations that scare you without succumbing to your fear.

Preparation is key here—you can't expect to quickly jump into real-life exposure. But with careful preparation, practice, and gradual exposure, you will be able to unlearn your fear. The methods in this chapter will help you do just that.

Three Deep Breaths and Good Preparation

When I was in high school, I was stricken with vicious stage fright, a form of performance anxiety, which is common for people with social anxiety. Waiting in the wings to go onstage, I would pray to God to make me fall over dead before I had to go out and sing. Dying may not have been the best choice of avoidance behaviors, but it was the only excuse the rest of the cast would accept if I missed my cue! My drama coach taught me one of the best anxiety management ideas I would ever learn. Intuitively creating diaphragmatic breathing because of her singing ability, she taught me to breathe slowly and deeply. She also taught me a cognitive framework for handling the anxiety, declaring, "All you need is three deep breaths and good preparation." Her "three deep breaths and good preparation" has become my model for getting rid of anxious behavior in any kind of anxiety-producing situation.

"Three deep breaths" stands for the ability to remain physically calm. It doesn't matter which breathing exercise you choose, or what kind of muscle relaxation you pair it with, as long as you use a physical calming technique when you face something that makes you anxious—ordering in a restaurant, speaking at a staff meeting, sitting in the middle of a theater, or driving on a toll road from which you can't exit for miles. Review Chapters 4 and 6 to refresh your memory on breathing and relaxation techniques. Also, listen to the track on the audio download, "5 Senses Centering Exercise," to help you stay cool and calm.

"Good preparation" stands for developing the competence to do what you want to do and developing the confidence to carry if off so that it ends in success—the key to memory reconsolidation. Having worked on your self-talk in Chapter 11 will be very useful for this. Changing your self-talk lays the groundwork for successfully using the methods discussed in this chapter.

Implement a Plan

Developing a solid plan involves getting motivated by setting goals, developing competence through skill-building, gaining confidence by practicing, and figuring out how to get real-life experience so that you can experience success. Take a look at Figure 12.1.

At the end of this section, you'll have a chance to fill out your own plan for an experience of memory reconsolidation. But first you need to learn the basics of setting goals, building skills, and practicing.

Set Goals

Why in the world would someone who wants to die rather than sing a solo in front of an audience go out to sing more than one time? Motivation! Once I got in front of the audience without dying, I enjoyed the act of singing. I had practiced it and I could do it well. I liked doing something I could do well. And then there was the

Figure 12.1 Plan to Reduce Anxiety

The 10 Best-Ever Anxiety Management Techniques Workbook

applause—it felt really good! With enough motivation, any person will face fear. And once you face your fear, it is diminished. I actually went on to major in speech and drama in college; learning that I could manage the fear and the motivation of loving the applause made that a desirable and doable choice.

Knowing what you stand to gain increases your motivation to face and overcome fear. It also helps you set goals. Setting goals solidifies motivation: when you can clearly see what you will have and feel like after accomplishing your goal, you will be more willing to try.

What are *your* goals? Are they something like these?

- To place an order in a restaurant without breaking into a sweat
- To speak to my boss without a quivering voice
- To stay in class this semester
- To start interviewing for jobs

Make a list of your goals. They can be very general or specific. But no matter how specific or general your goals are, your next step is to see if you have the skills necessary to achieve them.

Identify and Learn the Skills You Need

For those who avoid social experiences because they are afraid of panic, there is a prerequisite to real-life exposure. If your social or work life is impeded by fear of panic—such as being unable to work on upper levels of a building because you may panic in an elevator, or being afraid of working in a large space because you may feel panic when you are far from an exit—then controlling panic attacks is your first order of business. See Chapters 1 through 4 for controlling the physiology of anxiety. Then, if you need them, the rest of these skills will require your attention.

If you have social anxiety without panic, you may have social skills but feel very uncomfortable in social settings. Remember, *enjoying* doing something is not the same as being *able* to do it. For example, you may be able to smile, shake a stranger's hand, and say "It's nice to meet you" even if you don't particularly enjoy meeting new people. In other words, although you don't enjoy meeting new people, you *do* have the skills necessary to do it. You are competent to carry it off.

In identifying the skills you need, write down only the skills you actually *don't* have—don't include things you *can* do but don't *enjoy* doing.

The skills you will need depend on the kind of anxiety you have. Take a look at the following examples.

Social Skills

Check off each of the following items you *can't* do:

- ☐ Meet new people, introduce yourself, and ask questions of others
- ☐ Eat in public or eat with unfamiliar people at the table
- ☐ Speak in community meetings such as condo association or PTA
- ☐ Talk to teachers or administrative staff at your child's school
- ☐ Ask for a date or invite a new acquaintance to meet for coffee or lunch
- ☐ Other social skills: _____

_____

Personal–Business Skills

Check off each of the following items you *can't* do:

- ☐ Competently drive or use public transportation to get to work or social functions
- ☐ Run errands or shop for groceries or other necessities when stores are busy
- ☐ Be assertive enough to handle issues such as returning damaged goods or talking with customer-service representatives at banks or credit-card companies
- ☐ Ask questions of various services personnel about the cost of goods and services
- ☐ Sign checks or credit slips in front of a clerk
- ☐ Talk with retail personnel, asking questions about purchasing or ex-changing goods
- ☐ Talk with medical personnel and clarify information about medical conditions and treatments
- ☐ Deal with insurance companies for claims and coverage concerns (medical, home, auto, etc.)
- ☐ Talk with ease to your child's coaches or tutors or make appointments and financial arrangements for lessons
- ☐ Other personal business skills: _____

_____

Work or Career Skills

Check off each of the following items you *can't* do:

- ☐ Ask questions of a supervisor about your work duties
- ☐ Ask for training on a job task that you cannot perform adequately

☐ Attend training sessions with or without colleagues present

☐ Independently obtain additional training by finding and attending certification or education programs available in the community

☐ Discuss schedule-change requests with a manager

☐ Talk socially with a coworker at break

☐ Talk with a coworker about a work situation

☐ Enter a meeting room and choose where to sit in unstructured settings; greet colleagues as they enter the room

☐ Interview for a job

☐ Do what is necessary to make presentations at your job

☐ Offer comments during a group/committee meeting

☐ Other work or career skills: _____

_____

If you checked more than two items in any of these lists, you will need some basic skill-building in that area to dispense with anxiety. (If you *do* have the necessary skills and simply are not using them because you are avoiding situations, go ahead and skip the skill-building section that follows.)

Build Skills

It's very important to be honest with yourself about what you need to learn—you'll never become truly confident unless you have the competence (skills) to back it up. Once you've identified the skills you need, finding outside help to build them is the next step.

There are many ways to learn skills. If you already have a therapist, consult him or her first. You can also consider using workbooks for social-skills and assertiveness training. Several are listed in the Resources section of this workbook. You can also learn skills in group therapy, which is very useful for those with social anxiety because you are learning with others.

Groups are often available for learning specific skill sets, such as assertiveness, social skills, conflict management, and anger management. You may have to hunt to find a local therapist who offers these kinds of groups, but often it's well worth the effort. Look at adult-education departments at community colleges for topics like public speaking, flirting, interviewing, etiquette, and Internet communication, as well as for one-time social opportunities (such as tours or theater performances) that give you a chance to be social with a focus on the conversation. These classes are often very inexpensive.

Practice Beforehand

This part of the plan is about gaining *confidence*. Many people resist practicing, even in private, because they are embarrassed. That is exactly why it is necessary. Not practicing before the real event is akin to memorizing a part in a play but never saying it aloud before going onstage for the first performance. Not even a completely relaxed actor would want to go onstage without a rehearsal.

The best way to approach practice is to first break down your goals into smaller, achievable steps.

Identify Achievable Steps

You have already identified your goals. Some of them may be specific; others may be broader. For the ones that are broader, you need to break the goal down into smaller steps to improve your chances of achieving it.

For example, perhaps one of your goals was to learn to interview for jobs without looking nervous. This goal might be broken down into:

1. Be able to greet the people interviewing me
2. Be able to talk about myself
3. Be able to ask and answer questions without looking nervous

Go ahead and break your goal down into smaller steps.

My Goal: _____
Step #1 _____
Step #2 _____
Step #3 _____

Now, break those steps down into even smaller steps. Figure 12.2 is an example of how you might do that.

Identifying small steps that you can reasonably accomplish is the key to unlearning fear. Breaking off chunks too big for your temperament and skills is self-defeating. To ensure success in unlearning fear, make sure you can do each step before going on to the next one. Use the following form to break your goals down into the smallest steps possible.

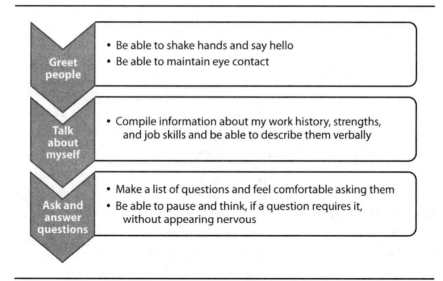

- Greet people
  - Be able to shake hands and say hello
  - Be able to maintain eye contact

- Talk about myself
  - Compile information about my work history, strengths, and job skills and be able to describe them verbally

- Ask and answer questions
  - Make a list of questions and feel comfortable asking them
  - Be able to pause and think, if a question requires it, without appearing nervous

Figure 12.2 Breaking Goals Down Into Achievable Steps

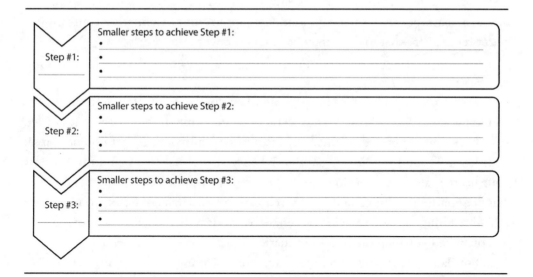

Step #1:
Smaller steps to achieve Step #1:
-
-
-

Step #2:
Smaller steps to achieve Step #2:
-
-
-

Step #3:
Smaller steps to achieve Step #3:
-
-
-

Now you're ready to begin practicing. It's best to find someone who will help you with this part of the plan.

Practice in Private—Not Real Life—and Get a Helper

You are going to need some practice to develop your confidence in your skills. To effectively do memory reconsolidation—reduce the impact of prior negative experiences—you won't go straight into a highly anxiety-provoking real-life practice. You must succeed at your goals, so practicing your skills first is the best way to approach this.

When you practice, your brain gets a workout that strengthens it to do the real work. The more often you practice, the better you will remember. You literally form connections in your brain that will make it easier to remember what you have practiced when you are under pressure. The more you run through what you want to say or do, the less sensitive you will be, and anxiety symptoms will be less likely to appear.

Who might be willing to help you practice your steps? It could be a parent, a therapist, a spouse or partner, or a friend. If you can't find someone to help you, be sure to at least speak your part out loud, perhaps in front of a mirror. Your lips will better remember what to do if they have said the words before.

Remember to Breathe During Practice

You're probably going to be nervous when you begin practicing, even though you know it's only a practice session. You may feel some shortness of breath or feel your heart start to pound. If this happens, just remind yourself that no one can see your heartbeat and that it will subside when you're done. You can diminish both your heart rate and your respiration by changing your breathing on purpose. Use diaphragmatic breathing, one-breath relaxation (see Chapter 6), or your favorite other breathing method to help you remain calm. It will also help you remember to breathe when you're in the real-life situation.

For example, suppose you are practicing speaking up at a staff meeting. To make the practice session as real as possible, you've decided to pretend that your dining room is the meeting room. You stand outside the dining room door and:

1. Feel yourself get tense as you imagine walking into the room.
2. Use one-breath relaxation as you walk through the door and again as you take a seat at the table. (This calms you.)
3. Feel yourself get tense again as you anticipate having to speak.

4. Use one-breath relaxation again to stay physically calm until it is time for you to speak. (This allows your body to remain as quiet as possible so your symptoms will not be easily triggered.)

5. Actually speak up, loosely following the script you planned ahead of time.

6. Use one-breath relaxation to calm yourself again immediately after speaking.

Now, when you go into the actual meeting, you will better remember when and how to breathe.

Rate Your Anxiety Level During Each Practice Session

Again, when you first begin practicing, you're probably going to be pretty nervous. As it turns out, that is necessary to change a bad memory. You want to activate any memory or expectation of failure so that your successful real-life practice will result in memory reconsolidation. The more you practice, the more competent and confident you'll become, ensuring your success.

Ensure Your Success

Staying calm enough to pull it off is necessary. You may fear that you will get so nervous you will flee. To develop confidence in your calmness, rate your anxiety level during each practice session. This is a way of being able to (1) visually see how your anxiety decreases and (2) get a sense of when you're ready to stop practicing and begin the real thing.

This method worked particularly well for Darius. Darius was an extremely shy young man, but he was also a reliable employee at the retail store where he worked. He wanted to take an accounting class that met on Saturday mornings at the community college, but his shift included weekends, and he knew his coworkers wouldn't be eager to trade shifts with him. He had told his manager when he was hired that he would be willing to work Saturdays, so now he felt very nervous about asking for this change. He wrote down what he wanted to say: "I know I agreed to work weekends, and I am still willing to work afternoons on Saturday. However, I want to advance my career, and this class is important to me. It only meets on Saturday morning. Will you please schedule me off Saturday mornings during this semester?"

He had only one shot to say this to the manager, so it was important that he get comfortable with his speech. He had a week to get ready, so he knew he'd better

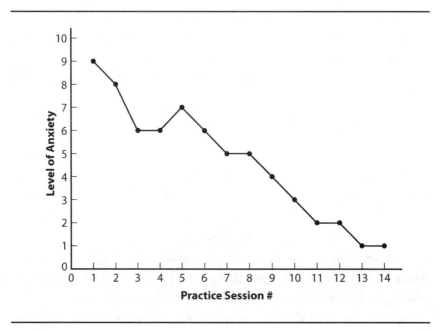

Figure 12.3 Level of Anxiety Over 14 Practice Sessions

practice a couple of times each day. He decided to do most of the practice sessions without help from a friend because he didn't want to "bore them," but he did agree to try it once with a friend for the practice session preceding the actual meeting.

Darius didn't expect to be completely calm when he talked to his manager, but he thought he could be "pretty calm"—maybe a 2. He wanted to be between 0 and 1 when he practiced with his friend. He used a graph like the one in Figure 12.3 to rate his anxiety during each of 14 practice sessions. As you can see, his anxiety level did indeed drop to a 1 by the 13th session and stayed at 1 during the 14th session with his friend.

If you are willing to have a session to learn how to use one of the versions of "tapping" (see Resources) to calm anticipatory anxiety, this may be a boon to all your anxiety management. It can't be taught in this book but wouldn't be hard for you to learn from a therapist who is trained to teach you.

Use the blank graph that follows Figure 12.3 to chart your own level of anxiety over the course of 14 practice sessions.

The 10 Best-Ever Anxiety Management Techniques Workbook

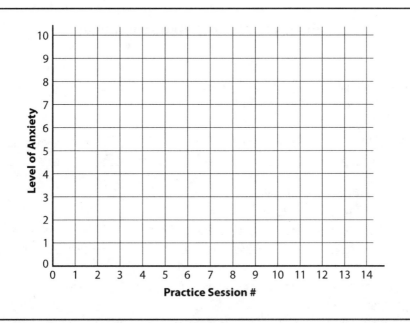

Recap

Let's go over your memory reconsolidation, anxiety-reduction plan one more time (Figure 12.4).

Of course, the specifics of each of these steps will depend on what kind of goal you have set. Take a look at the following example of a mother who wants to be able to take her kids to the movies without having a panic attack.

Anxiety-Reduction Plan

1. Set goals
2. Identify the skills you need
3. Build skills
4. Practice beforehand
   - Identify achievable steps
   - Break down steps into even smaller steps
   - Get a helper
   - Remember to breathe
   - Rate your anxiety level during each practice session

Figure 12.4 Anxiety-Reduction Plan

Example Anxiety-Reduction Plan

What is my goal? *I want to go to the movies with my kids.*

Do I have the skills to do this? *Yes—I used to go to the movies before I started panicking in movie theaters.*

How will I build skills to do this? *I don't need skill-building in this case because going to the movies doesn't require anything I don't know how to do.*

My plan to practice beforehand:
- *I will go to a movie alone so I don't bother my kids if I blow it.*
- *I will get to the theater a few hours ahead of the show so I have time to buy tickets and look around. Then I'll run some errands before coming back for the movie.*
- *I'll get to the theater early so I can sit where I am comfortable. I'll breathe and relax.*
- *I will get up, walk out, and then return during the previews—a time when I know no one will be bothered by my practicing leaving and returning in the dark.*
- *If I get nervous I have my reminder to breathe panic away. If I feel I need to leave to calm down, I will reenter the theater and sit down again to show myself I can.*
- *I will repeat the above experience to be sure I am confident before I take the kids.*

What are my anxiety-level ratings? *The first time I tried this, my anxiety was so high that I didn't return to the theater again after buying tickets. The second time, I was able to follow through on the whole plan—my anxiety was high (an 8) but I managed to get through it. The third time, my anxiety started at a 5, but by the time the movie was over I'd almost forgotten that this was a practice session, and when I left the theater my anxiety was 0.*

Figure 12.5 Example Anxiety-Reduction Plan

The 10 Best-Ever Anxiety Management Techniques Workbook

DESENSITIZATION OF TRAUMA

Developing your confidence in how the real-life situation will go may depend on desensitizing yourself to the feared situation. The plan described in this chapter works very well for people whose anxiety is *not* rooted in earlier trauma. There *are* valuable desensitization techniques for people who have suffered trauma, but they require help from a therapist and can't be taught in a workbook. Some of these treatments include systematic desensitization, eye movement desensitization and reprocessing (EMDR), Rapid Resolution Therapy (RRT), "tapping" energy therapy that goes by several names, and brain-spotting. See the Resources section for information on how to find these therapies. These can be excellent choices to help with desensitizing, especially if you have a history of having been shamed, bullied, humiliated, or terrified. It is not easy to bounce back from such life experiences without additional help.

The process of memory reconsolidation occurs during many of the above therapies because they fit the reconsolidation model of negative arousal, successfully seeing the outcome in a positive light, and integrating new information into the memory of the trauma.

REAL-LIFE PRACTICE

Once you have identified what you want to do, developed competence (learned skills), and improved your confidence by practicing in private, now it's time to get out into real life. Real-life practice must end in success, so start with small steps you feel confident of achieving. These should gradually increase the length of time you spend in the situation to allow you to leave while still feeling calm or should gradually increase the complexity of the social experience. This is how you will unlearn your fear—achieve memory reconsolidation.

Theater actors prepare for performances by going through several exposures of increasing intensity—a process that serves as a good metaphor for anxiety reduction. After rehearsing their lines in a practice room or other space, actors get on stage to know where to stand (that's like the desensitization stage of your plan). Then there is a technical rehearsal in which actors wear their costumes and the crew tests whether lights, music, curtains, and scene changes work smoothly. No one is in the audience, even though this is conducted just like the real thing. Then comes the dress rehearsal, usually with a small audience of people connected to the perform-

---

Real-Life Practice

What is my goal?   *I want to go to happy hour on Friday with my coworkers.*

Do I have the skills to socialize?   *I have practiced making small talk about work, the weather, and local sports teams. I think I am ready.*

My real-life practice sessions:
- *Stay first for 30 minutes.*
- *Then stay 60 minutes the next time, but without ordering food, so I won't worry about eating with them.*
- *Then I will order food, and stay until I have eaten at least some of it.*
- *After that, I will stay until the group breaks up for the evening.*

What are my anxiety-level ratings?   *My anxiety stayed at about an 8 during the first real-life practice session. It was actually higher during the next session when everyone ordered food, but when I saw that no one even noticed that I wasn't eating with them, it went down to a 7. During the next session it was at a 6. It got a little higher when I ordered food, but went back down again after I'd eaten a couple of bites and then let the waitress clear the plate. In the last session it was at a 4, even while we all ate. I'm pretty sure it'll be even lower the next time.*

Figure 12.6 Real-Life Practice

ers and some of the crew. In professional theater, there are low-cost "preview performances" while the little mistakes are ironed out. Your real-life practices are the equivalent of these rehearsals. Just like with the tech and dress rehearsals that few people will even see, be sure you start out with steps that have minor consequences for either success or failure. For example, if you fear driving on the highway, don't start by getting on the road during rush hour in a downpour. Rather, go out on a clear Sunday morning and ride a short distance and go home. The next time you drive, go a bit farther or get on a limited-access road for a mile or two. Then try it when there will be more traffic and so on.

The most difficult part of this technique is getting exactly the right degree of exposure that uses your competence and guarantees you can succeed. Just like with the practice sessions, you will use a graph to rate your level of anxiety during each real-life exposure. If you see your anxiety level go down with each subsequent real-life practice session, you know you've achieved the right degree of exposure. If it begins an upward trend, you need to think about taking smaller steps. Use the graph on page 223 to rate your anxiety over 14 real-life practice sessions.

Figure 12.6 shows an example of setting up the real-life practice. In this example, a man with social anxiety wants to be able to go to happy hour with his coworkers.

Remember: It Won't Always Go Perfectly

What happens if you fail or get anxious while making a small step? Be grateful! This is a great opportunity to evaluate what kinds of things trip you up and to review and adjust your plan so that you get better and better. Whatever you do, don't dwell on it or tell yourself bad things about yourself. Everyone makes mistakes. Have some reasonable expectations (Figure 12.7).

Don't Sweat It!

- The process reveals what else you need to know. If something goes wrong, it will just give you a better sense of what you have to plan for.
- Everyone makes mistakes. No one is exempt. You are human.
- Failing to achieve what you wanted in the step is no big deal—you have been scared or embarrassed before, and it didn't kill you. Your brain is accustomed to it. It will be possible to try again with a better plan.

Figure 12.7 Don't Sweat It!

FROM IMPLEMENTING A PLAN TO REAL-LIFE PRACTICE: A RECAP

The idea behind this technique is that fear is driven by the whole-body remembering of negative experiences, including the heart-pounding, red-faced, stomach-churning sensations as well as the negative thoughts. When that network of memory is activated, it can be changed by being in a situation that could raise that degree of negative arousal but then having a good experience—completely mismatching what you expected to happen.

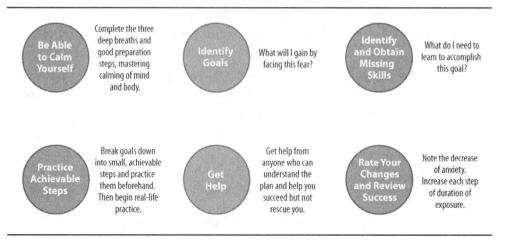

Figure 12.8 From Implementing a Plan to Real-Life Practice

It is necessary to ensure you will succeed, because success paves the way for more success. This is how your brain unlearns fear—every time you are able to do something without getting panicky or embarrassed, the emotional part of your brain says, "Hey, wait! I thought that would be dangerous, but I guess I was wrong. Apparently, I *don't* always have to send out a warning the next time I'm in that situation." And even if you *do* get panicked or embarrassed, seeing that you can live through it also helps change your expectation of what it means to face a challenge of being panicky or embarrassed—"I survived without disaster!" The whole process—from implementing a plan to real-life practice—is shown in Figure 12.8.

Remember that you will keep building on your successes until the whole goal is met. At every stage, the new learning (or unlearning of fear) lays groundwork for the next step to occur safely. It isn't until the whole goal is met that the safe experience will completely turn off the warning signal for that specific situation in the future.

A FINAL WORD

This is the one chapter that doesn't easily lend itself to a S.I.M.P.L.E. plan because of the number of steps that planning for exposure requires. That is why there is so much emphasis on planning small steps and evaluating their success. Preparing by implementing a plan and practicing are the keys to "being there without scare" and

The 10 Best-Ever Anxiety Management Techniques Workbook

unlearning fear. Practice means exactly that: making trial runs to do things you haven't been able to do before. And no one goes out on a practice run without preparation. If you are preparing for an athletic event, you learn skills, get advice about how to do those skills, try them out, see what works and what doesn't, and then try them out again before the competition. Practicing the three Cs—calmness, competence, and confidence—can be done by setting goals, learning skills, and practicing so you can go out into real life as a success. Practice makes possible.

Resources

The options for excellent information obtainable over the Internet abound. They also change frequently and new resources are added at a remarkable pace. Therefore the lists here are subject to change, but are at least a place to start :

Apps for Mobile Devices:

The Anxiety Depression Association of America (www.adaa.org) provides a review of new mobile apps that you might find helpful. Likewise, an excellent resource from Northwestern University is Intellicare – a review of mental health apps for all conditions: From the website: "IntelliCare is a suite of apps that work together to target common causes of depression and anxiety like sleep problems, social isolation, lack of activity, and obsessive thinking. These apps are part of a nationwide research study funded by the National Institutes of Health. Download individual apps or the whole IntelliCare suite from the Google Play Store."

And here are some that have been around a while that I like.

Breathing:
- Breathe2relax
- Mycalmbeat
- Relaxlite

Worry:
- Mindshift
- SAMApp
- Breathing Bubbles

Meditation:
- Calm
- Headspace
- Simply Being

Sleep :
- CBTi Coach for sleeping better

Websites

There are several helpful websites for mental-health resources, including those of the major universities and treatment facilities where research and training occur.

National websites related to mental health include:
- Anxiety and Depression Association of America: www.adaa.org
- American Psychiatric Association: www.psychiatry.org
- American Psychological Association: www.apa.org
- International Obsessive Compulsive Disorder Foundation : www .iocdf.org
- National Library of Medicine: www.medlineplus.gov
- National Alliance for the Mentally Ill: www.nami.org
- Substance Abuse and Mental Health Services Administration: www .samhsa.gov

Websites for Psychotherapy
- Aaron Beck offers tools and resources for cognitive therapy: www. beckinstitute.org
- David Burns focuses on depression as well as anxiety and has many resources at: www.feelinggood.com
- For more about Albert Ellis and rational emotive behavior therapy (REBT): www.rebt.org
- For links to many websites with information about REBT and national organizations for REBT, including addiction work: www.rebt network.org/links.html
- Mindfulness is one of the most rapidly growing arenas of help for all forms of psychological healing. Jon Kabat-Zinn is a leading developer

of a program called the Mindfulness Based Stress Reduction (MBSR) program at the University of Massachusetts Medical Center: www .umassmed.edu/cfm

- Daniel Siegel is a major contributor to teaching therapists the benefits and techniques of using mindfulness for healing: www.drdansiegel .com

Sleep Better
- American Academy of Sleep Medicine www.aasmnet.org had significant information about sleep disorders.
- If you want ideas to sleep better, consult www.sleepeducation.com, which is sponsored by the American Academy of Sleep Medicine. It is a terrific education site to give you all the ideas you need to follow to make you sleep work for reducing your anxiety.

Herbal Medicine and Supplements
There are several excellent commercial websites that offer good information about herbs and supplements, and in the bibliography you will find some books on the topic. This is a not-for-profit site: The American Botanical Council. From their website: "At the American Botanical Council, we are passionate about helping people live healthier lives through the responsible use of herbs, medicinal plants. We are an independent, nonprofit research and education organization dedicated to providing accurate and reliable information for consumers, healthcare practitioners, researchers, educators, industry and the media."
PO Box 144345
Austin, TX 78714-4345
Phone: 512-926-4900
Toll free: 800-373-7105
Fax: 512-926-2345
http://abc.herbalgram.org

Guided Imagery and Relaxation Audio CD's:
Sources on You Tube provide an endless array of choices for guided meditation and relaxation.

You can check out some of the authors' websites who also offer guided meditation: Barbara Frederickson, Jon Kabat-Zinn, Kristin Neff, Daniel Siegel.

Resources for Social Skills

Bradberry, T., & Greaves, J. (2009). *Emotional intelligence 2.0.* Available at Amazon.

Childre, D., & Rozman, D. (2008). *Transforming anxiety: The HeartMath solution for overcoming fear and worry and creating serenity.* Oakland, CA: New Harbinger.

Cooper, B., & Widdows, N. (2008). *Social success workbook for teens: Skill-building activities for teens with nonverbal learning disorder, Asperger disorder and other social-skill problems.* Oakland, CA: Instant Help/New Harbinger.

Crowe K. (2017). *There is no good card for this: What to say and do when life is scary, awful, and unfair to people you love.* New York: HarperOne.

Duhigg, C. (2012). *The power of habit: Why we do what we do in business and life.* New York: Random House.

MacLeod, C. (2016). *The social skills guidebook: Manage shyness, improve your conversations, and make friends.* Self-published; available at Amazon.

Robbins, M.J. (2002). *Acting techniques in everyday life.* New York: Marlowe.

Thaler, R., & Sunstein, C. (2008). *Nudge: Improving decision about health, wealth, and happiness.* New Haven, CT: Yale University Press.

Other Therapies

Learn more about EMDR

From the Website, "EMDR International Association (EMDRIA) is a professional association[...]committed to assuring that therapists are knowledgeable and skilled in the methodology of EMDR [...]. This website provides information and services to the greater EMDR community including clinicians, researchers, and the public that our members serve." *Scott Blech, CAE, Executive Director* EMDRIA

EMDR International Association
5806 Mesa Drive, Suite 360
Austin, Texas 78731
Tel: 512-451-5200 Toll Free in the US: 866-451-5200
Fax: 512-451-5256
Email: info@emdria.org

Learn more about energy therapies:

Emotional Freedom Technique, EFT, PO Box 269, Coulterville, CA 95311, www.emofree.com

Fred Gallo and Harry Vincenzi Energy Tapping Information at www.energypsych .com

George Pratt and Peter Lambrou and Instant Emotional Healing Information at http://www.instantemotionalhealing.com

Learn about Rapid Resolution Therapy

Founded by Jon Connelly, Rapid Resolution Therapy utilizes precise hypnotic communication therapy techniques to resolve trauma: www.rapidresolutionther apy.com

Index